AWAITING
THE
ALREADY

AWAITING THE ALREADY

An Advent Journey Through the Gospels

❄

MAGREY R. DEVEGA

An Advent Study for Adults

Abingdon Press / Nashville

AWAITING THE ALREADY
An Advent Journey Through the Gospels
BY MAGREY R. DEVEGA

Library of Congress Cataloging-in-Publication Data

DeVega, Magrey R.
    Awaiting the already : an Advent journey through the gospels / Magrey
R. deVega. -- First [edition].
        pages cm
    "An Advent study for adults."
    Includes bibliographical references and index.
    ISBN 978-1-5018-0089-4 (pbk. : alk. paper) 1. Advent--Biblical
teaching. 2. Bible. Gospels--Criticism, interpretation, etc. I. Title.
    BV40.D475 2015
    242'.332--dc23

                                                    2015015402

ISBN-13: 9781501800894

15 16 17 18 19 20 21 22 23 24—10 9 8 7 6 5 4 3 2 1

Manufactured in the United States of America

To Rich, Andrea, John, and Jan, for giving me the gift of Advent Hope;

To Jim and Celia, for generously sharing gifts of Advent Peace;

To my parents, brothers, and their families, for their unconditional Advent Love;

And to Grace and Madelyn, for filling my life with constant Advent Joy.

CONTENTS

INTRODUCTION   9

First Week of Advent
MARK: Slow Down, Pay Attention   13

Second Week of Advent
MATTHEW: The World As It Is   31

Third Week of Advent
LUKE: The Ultimate Advent Playlist   47

Fourth Week of Advent
JOHN: The Light in the Darkness   65

Christmas
TITUS: Paul's Christmas Letter   81

INTRODUCTION

Advent Bible studies don't generally begin with a story about swimming in a sunny water park. But Advent is no ordinary season.

A few years ago, I took my two daughters to a water park down in Florida. To capture the memories without jeopardizing my camera phone, I purchased a waterproof, disposable camera, with an attached rubber strap that I could wrap around my wrist.

I can't remember the last time I took a photograph with an old-fashioned film camera, one that did not have some kind of display screen. I have grown so accustomed to seeing the photo the instant I take it that it took me several shots before I stopped looking at the back side of the camera to see how the picture looked. I used up all twenty-seven exposures, capturing images of the girls and me cruising down the water slides, floating on the lazy river, and rafting along some rapids. With each click of the camera, I wondered how the pictures would eventually turn out.

It took me the remainder of our trip to Florida—and even several days after we got back—before I could find a place that would develop the pictures. Having waited that long already, I opted for the express, one-hour service. There was no way I was going to wait any more days to see those pictures.

We have steadily removed the need to wait in our culture, haven't we? We have proven over and over that we will invent just about anything to reduce how long we have to wait for something to happen. In so doing, we have also diminished those moments of richness and fullness that only come with anticipation.

But I do think there is something different about waiting for camera film to develop. That experience carries a unique tension between the past and the future, between an event that has already taken place, and a forthcoming reliving of that moment. Riding on the water slides with the girls had occurred weeks before, yet I was still eager for the store photo processor to hand me those pictures so I could see those memories in a fresh, new way.

I once thought Advent made things too complicated. Why do we have to spend four weeks pretending that Jesus has not yet been born, when we know full well that he has? After all, advertisers and retailers would want us to believe that the Christmas season is already here. So why prepare for something that has already happened?

Maybe Advent is a lot like waiting for pictures to develop. Of all the seasons in the Christian year, it best captures the dynamic tension between the past and the future, in a way that fills us with hopeful anticipation in the present. When we journey to Bethlehem, it's not that we think Jesus has not been born, and it's not just that we believe Jesus will come again. It is about opening a freshly developed set of photographs, and allowing the past and the future to amaze us again in the present, as if the arrival of Jesus were happening for the very first time. Advent is not a time of pretending that Jesus has never been born; it is a time of preparing for what that birth might mean for us today. It is not a denial, but a darkroom: a chance to allow the fullness of God's love to develop in our lives and to be revealed in glorious Technicolor.

Over the course of this study, we will traverse familiar territory, hearing the stories we have heard countless times over the years. The photographers, if you will, of our journey are the four Gospel writers, who each assume a different angle on the action, panning, zooming, and selectively choosing which parts of the birth narrative best convey their message. Altogether, these stories form one of the essential narratives of our faith: the anticipation and arrival of the Word Made Flesh.

But if we keep them separated in their respective Gospels, we discover some unique lessons that each author would have us learn about awaiting the Word:

- Mark would want us to slow down, turn around, and prepare the way for Jesus.
- Matthew would want us to confront, rather than ignore, the realities of this hurting world, and to look for the Jesus who is already here.
- Luke would want us to sing—songs of obedience, of praise, and even of silence.
- John would want us to see the light in the midst of our darkness, and become a gift for others.

By the end of our study, you will have a better knowledge of what parts of the Christmas story come from which Gospel. And you will be better able to resolve the oddness of Advent, waiting for a Christ who is already here. But more importantly, you will be equipped to enter this season fully prepared to receive Christ in a fresh, new way.

When the clerk handed me my photographs, I tore into the envelope like a child ripping open a Christmas gift. I had not even paid for the pictures yet before I began to relive each ride, each memory, each thrilling occasion for laughter and joy, in a way that made the past alive again.

That "thrill of hope" can only come from waiting. So, brothers and sisters, welcome to Advent. Let's await the already together.

MARK

John the Baptist
"Slow Down, Pay Attention"

READ: MARK 1:1-8

There is nothing about the Gospel of Mark that is slow. It moves along at a brisk clip, covering the necessary details of Jesus' life like a sports highlight reel. Mark's favorite word is *immediately* or *straightaway*: The Greek word for *immediately* occurs forty-one times in Mark, three times as much as the other three Gospels combined. The rest of Mark's writing style shows his concern for haste too. Whereas Matthew and Luke fill their Gospels with more of Jesus' teachings, and John is replete with poetic flourish and vivid imagery, Mark is all about action.

It's the shortest of the Gospels, and widely regarded to be the first one written. That's why we will consider it here first, rather than Matthew. Mark's version broke into the scene and formed the basis for the later Gospel portraits of Jesus. So to do a comprehensive survey of the four accounts of Jesus' birth, it is best to start here and see what Mark has to say about the birth of Jesus. And it turns out that Mark says . . . nothing.

It might be odd that for an event as significant in human history as the Incarnation of God's own Son, the earliest portrait we have of it is like a blank canvas. There are no angels, no shepherds, no mention of Mary or Joseph, no star, and no manger. Instead, when we first meet Jesus in the Gospel's ninth verse, he is already a grown man.

So why include Mark in this four-dimensional portrait of Advent? Because this Gospel—this brisk, fast-paced, action-packed thriller of a Gospel—begins in a way that is not only unique among the four Gospels. It leads with a message that is quintessentially Advent.

Mark begins right off the bat with John the Baptist. Matthew and Luke don't talk about John's ministry until their respective third chapters. The Book of John reports John the Baptist's ministry only after a lengthy, poetic discourse about Jesus. But Mark? He begins with a starter's pistol, a firecracker, a voice from the wilderness that begins the story in the most attention-grabbing, eye-catching way.

It is as if Mark, with pen and paper in hand, is writing the equivalent of police sirens and flashing lights. He wants to get your attention.

Slow Down, Pay Attention

One day after I picked up my two daughters from school, we headed over to run some errands in a city about an hour away. The girls settled in the back seat for the long drive, watching a movie on their movie player, while I spent the time working through the myriad of items on my mental checklist: follow-up work on Commitment Sunday, preparations for a big upcoming funeral, Advent starting the upcoming Sunday—all in a shortened work week. Check, check, check.

I don't know how long I had been driving before I noticed the flashing blue and red lights. When the officer approached me, I still had no idea why I had been pulled over.

"Do you know how fast you were going?" he asked me. Well, that answered why he had pulled me over. I thought about saying, "You have no idea how fast I've been moving today." I wanted to show him my to-do list, my day planner, and my e-mail inbox. Take a radar gun to that, I thought to myself.

When he told me how fast I was going, I knew there was no squirming out of it. My older daughter Grace, who was only seven at the time, looked up from her movie to notice what was happening and frantically asked:

"DADDY, IS HE GOING TO TAKE YOU TO JAIL?"

The officer chuckled and took my license back to the squad car, as I said to her, "Don't give him any ideas."

Of course, speeding was just a symptom of the deeper problem. I had become absorbed by the world inside my head instead of focusing on the road. And it took flashing lights and a badge to shock me back to reality.

This is what Mark's Advent narrative offers for us. In a Gospel that would become very fast moving, and to an audience that would be moving even faster, John the Baptist bursts onto the scene as a voice crying in the wilderness, as sirens blaring in the rear view mirror, to get us to pay attention, slow down, and change our behavior.

You and I enter the Advent season every year with nearly the same mentality.

- We live in an artificial world of our own construction, rather than a world that invites us into the mysteries of faith and trust.

- We're stuck in a pressurized world of deadlines and instantaneous results, rather than a lifelong commitment to gradual maturity.
- We're speeding through a world jaded by cynicism and worry, instead of embracing a world of imagination and possibility.
- We might even say we're not quite ready for Christmas or Advent yet. And that's precisely the point. We're not ready for God to break into our lives, because we are too busy living in our own self-made world.
- And when we think we are ready for Advent, we jump right to the good stuff, the stuff in Matthew, Luke, and John. We'd prefer placid scenes of hillside shepherds, starry nights, and lowing cattle. We cling to these images because they offer us a kind of anesthetizing nostalgia back to days before life became so chaotic and so confusing.

The last thing we want—and the last thing we expect—is an Advent message from Mark. And there's a reason that the message of John the Baptist can be found in the second week of Advent every year, no matter what lectionary year we're on in the church.

These words read like flashing blue and red lights in your rear view mirror. "Pull over! Keep alert! Snap out of it! You're drifting off into a different reality rather than the one that is set before you." They grab our attention in order to recalibrate us toward what is most important about the season. Get ready for the Messiah. Change your behavior. And ask God for forgiveness.

This may not be the way we expect to start our Advent journey, but it's the way we need to start it. We need once again to surrender to the mystery, the complexity, and the wonder of the Incarnation. And so very often, that involves a dramatic, urgent shout to wake us from our absorption with the world we've made.

Preparing the Way

Now, while all four Gospels include the story of John the Baptist and overlap in their essential ingredients, Mark highlights a certain aspect of John's message in a way the other three do not. Two times in his introduction of John, Mark uses the word *prepare* in his quotation from Isaiah: "Look, I am sending my messenger before you. He will prepare your way, a voice shouting in the wilderness: 'Prepare the way for the Lord; make his paths straight'" (Mark 1:2-3). Actually, Mark quotes two different prophets here, though he only mentions Isaiah. The second part of the quotation, in verse 3, is from Isaiah 40:3. The first part, in verse 2, comes from Malachi 3:1. Both of these prophetic messages are understood throughout the Gospels to be fulfilled in the person of John the Baptist. But only in Mark do they occur side by side.

At first glance, it might seem that Mark is being redundant. Grammar teachers and book editors might fault him for using the same word twice within a hairsbreadth of each other. Maybe that is why Matthew and Luke, in their versions, separate these two instances of *prepare* by several chapters. In Matthew, the Isaiah prophecy shows up in Matthew 3:3 and the Malachi prophecy in Matthew 11:10. Luke quotes the Isaiah passage in Luke 3:4 and the Malachi passage in Luke 7:27.

But before we break out the red pen to start correcting Mark, we should remember that the author wrote in Greek, not English. When we dig a little deeper, we discover that the Greek uses two different words for *prepare* in Mark 1:2-3. And that nuance in translation makes a big difference.

The first word for prepare ("He will prepare your way") is a Greek word that can also mean construct or create as well as furnish or equip. It often has the sense of making a building, vessel, or object ready for use. The Bible often uses this word or its derivatives to describe the preparation of household goods, containers, and other kinds of commonplace items. But in the New Testament it also describes the building of the Tabernacle and Noah's ark, important vessels that are associated with God's deliverance and presence (Hebrews 9:1-7; 1 Peter 3:20). In a sense, this word for prepare can mean to make human beings ready as vessels, receptacles of God's love, compassion, and grace.

In other words, Mark uses the first word for *prepare* to say, "Make yourself ready to be the vessel through which God's love can enter into human history."

How does John the Baptist call people to be prepared? He will be the voice crying out in the wilderness to prepare the way for the Lord. Here Mark uses the second Greek word for prepare, which often has the sense of "get ready for a big event." It involves making something ready in anticipation of what will happen later. Frequently in the New Testament, the word describes the great, heavenly future God has prepared for those who love him and follow Jesus (John 14:2-3; 1 Corinthians 2:9; Hebrews 11:16). Throughout the Gospels, that word is used to describe the imminence of a great wedding or banquet feast, or even what will happen at the second coming of Jesus (Matthew 22:4; 25:34, 41). But what Matthew, Mark, and Luke all have in common is that they use that word to describe Jesus' and the disciples' preparations for the Passover and the Last Supper (Matthew 26:17-19; Mark 14:12-16; Luke 22:7-13). In Mark's words: "On the first day of the Festival of Unleavened Bread, when the Passover lamb was sacrificed, the disciples said to Jesus,

'Where do you want us to prepare for you to eat the Passover meal?'" (Mark 14:12).

The Passover meal was the yearly Jewish celebration in which the people remembered their deliverance from slavery in Egypt. Christians remember that meal as the Last Supper, because it was the final meal that Jesus shared with his disciples before his betrayal, arrest, and crucifixion. It would be in that sacred meal that Jesus would prepare his disciples for his death and point them toward the future when all of the mysteries of salvation would be revealed. It would be in and through the remembrance of his sacrificial gift for the world that the disciples would be able to participate, in dynamic and real fashion, in his ongoing presence in the world.

By calling us to prepare the way of the Lord through John the Baptist, Mark challenges us to change our hearts and lives and make ourselves ready to receive Jesus, along with everything that entails. He calls us to adopt hearts and lives characterized by a desire to follow Jesus, a willingness to suffer on account of him, and a hope in the glorious future life he has promised us.

So, here is what Mark does in just those first few verses of his Gospel. By using two different aspects of the word *prepare*, he is calling his audience to 1) make themselves ready as vessels or homes to receive Jesus and 2) participate sacramentally in Jesus' life, death, and resurrection.

Living Sacramentally, Remembering Dynamically

Jesus' last meal with his disciples in the upper room is an event recorded in all four Gospels, and it introduces an enduring ritual in the life and liturgy of the early church

(Matthew 26:17-30; Mark 14:12-26; Luke 22:7-30; John 13:1-20). The breaking of bread and the sharing of the cup became the chief mode through which the earliest Christians could remember Jesus Christ (1 Corinthians 11:23-26). And today Communion is at the heart of what it means to remember what Jesus did for us.

Jesus told his disciples to remember him each time they shared the Communion bread and wine, and whenever we celebrate Communion in the church we recall Jesus' instructions to "*do this in remembrance of me*" (Luke 22:19). But what does it mean exactly to "do this in remembrance of" Jesus? And how is that remembrance an essential key to anticipating the arrival of a Jesus who is already here?

When the New Testament speaks of remembrance, it often uses the Greek word *anamnesis*, a word packed with so much meaning that there is no perfect English equivalent. To first-century Christians, this kind of remembering was more than just "fondly recollecting," or flipping back through one's mental scrapbook to ponder past events. To remember something "anamnetically" was to recall with such vividness and clarity that the events of the past come alive in the present, as if they were happening for the first time. It is exactly what happened when I opened those water park photographs to relive those summer memories with my two daughters.

This concept might be hard for our modern minds to comprehend, though it is an important idea in Christian theology. How can something in the past be relived so vividly that it is happening in the present? Science fiction and fantasy movies have toyed with the idea. Fans of *Star Trek: The Next Generation* might think about the holodeck on the starship Enterprise. Others may recall the *pensieve*, through which Albus Dumbledore stores and relives vivid memories with Harry in the *Harry Potter* films. Still others might even think of the time-jumping antics of Marty McFly in the *Back to the Future* movies. In each case, the person in the present relives the past with such a real experience that the lines between past and present are almost blurred.

That is what it means for United Methodists to believe in the "real presence" of Christ among us when we celebrate Communion. When we break the bread and share the cup, we not only remember what Christ did, but we acknowledge that Christ is doing it again in the present.

This is what Jesus meant in the upper room at the Last Supper, when he told his disciples to share in the bread and the cup "in remembrance" of him. When we partake of Communion, we aren't just retelling a fable secured in the distant past. We remember "anamnetically," sharing such a dynamic remembrance of Jesus that he is actually alive in our experience, a real presence in real time.

But here's part two. Another important aspect of Christian remembering is *prolepsis*. Whereas *anamnesis* is a dynamic remembrance of the past, *prolepsis* is a remembrance of the *future*. Prolepsis is a vivid type of anticipation, experiencing in the present a reality that we expect in the future.

Now talk about mind-blowing. When we gather around the Communion table, we not only observe what Jesus did for us two thousand years ago, we also live out in the present moment the very future God has promised for us and our world. United Methodists include in their Communion liturgy these words as the closing prayer of the Great Thanksgiving: "By your Spirit make us one with Christ, one with each other, and one in ministry to all the world, until Christ comes in final victory and we feast at his heavenly banquet."[1]

To prepare for the coming of Jesus once again in our lives is to live out the presence of Christ among us, right here and right now. To await Jesus is to acknowledge the Jesus who is already in our midst, and to fully live into his life, death, and resurrection.

If these kinds of time-shifting, mind-altering ideas are too much for us grasp all at once, that's okay. That's one of the reasons the church, over its history, has developed patterns of worship and sacred places to ground our lives in our experience of God's holy timing. Consider all these aspects of our worship and how they help us experience the past and the future as present realities:

- When we speak together the words of the Lord's Prayer, our voices join with the saints who have gone before us. Their witness to the power of prayer is alive among us in the present moment.
- When we speak in unison the Apostles' Creed, we testify to the very faith codified by the sacrifice of our ancestors. We affirm the "communion of saints" and the "life everlasting" as a future promise we can claim today.
- When we gather at the Communion table or the baptismal font, we can attest to the presence of a "great cloud of witnesses." Saints around the world and from long ago join us in that sacred experience.
- When we sing the hymns of the church, including the carols of Christmas, we can hear the melodies and harmonies of all of those who have sung those words, claimed those promises, and turned to those songs for hope, comfort, and conviction.
- When we read and study the words of Scripture, we can feel the heartbeat of those whose lifeblood was nourished by the ancient texts, in which they found the courage to face their futures unafraid.
- And when we journey through the seasons of the year, particularly during Advent, we believe that we are

accompanied by those who have traversed this path before us, along with those who will follow us long after we are gone.

Mark is unique in the way he uses two different words for *prepare* to describe the work of John the Baptist at the beginning of his Gospel. Together, they remind us that to be prepared for the arrival of Jesus requires the inner work of confession and repentance, as well as the anticipatory work of participating in the sacraments.

It should be no wonder that moments after John makes this public declaration, he calls people to baptism, one of the two sacraments that United Methodists and most other Protestants recognize. When we observe a baptism of a new person in Christ, we are participating together in the death, burial, and triumphant resurrection of Jesus. We not only recall his death on the cross, and we not only anticipate his glorious return; we share in the new life today that God's past faithfulness and promised future afford us. We await the already.

Mark's use of *prepare* is a central aspect of both baptism, at the beginning of Jesus' life, and Communion, at the end of Jesus' life. It is a critical means by which followers of Jesus can be prepared for his presence at the beginning (baptism) and throughout the ongoing (communion) journey of Christian discipleship.

Walking Straight

But while Mark is the only one to use the word *prepare* twice at the beginning of his Gospel, here is where all the Gospel writers agree: The best way to prepare for the arrival of Jesus is to make his paths straight. All the Gospel writers quote Isaiah 40:3 in reference to John the Baptist, where the prophet uses this language of *straight paths for the Lord.*

It should be no wonder to us that all four Gospels use that terminology, since the imagery of a straight path to describe the holy and righteous life is quite common throughout the Bible.

In Proverbs, the teacher instructs all who wish to live the right kind of life by telling them:

> Focus your eyes straight ahead;
>   keep your gaze on what is in front of you.
> Watch your feet on the way,
>   and all your paths will be secure.
> Don't deviate a bit to the right or the left;
>   turn your feet away from evil (Proverbs 4:25-27).

Then, writing centuries later, the author of Hebrews gives a similar image:

> No discipline is fun while it lasts, but it seems painful at the time. Later, however, it yields the peaceful fruit of righteousness for those who have been trained by it.
>   So strengthen your drooping hands and weak knees! Make straight paths for your feet so that if any part is lame, it will be healed rather than injured more seriously. Pursue the goal of peace along with everyone—and holiness as well, because no one will see the Lord without it (Hebrews 12:11-14).

In other words, if you want to prepare a way for Jesus that leads to true, abundant, and holy living, then that path must be in a straight line! You can't deviate to the left or the right, you can't choose to go your own way for part of the time, and you can't stop to smell the roses. Preparing oneself for the imminent arrival of Jesus means continuing to move forward, step by step, sacrifice by sacrifice, in anticipation of a God who will become real in Jesus. That is easier said than done, of course, since most of the time, we are prone to going our own way. Left on our own, we simply cannot walk in a straight line.

It's true. Human beings are unable to walk in a straight line on their own. There is just something about our inner orientation that causes us to walk in a crooked or warped way. That's the conclusion of Robert Krulwich, science correspondent for NPR. In an interview on *Morning Edition*, Krulwich spoke with Jan Souman, a scientist from Germany who has studied the phenomenon. Souman blindfolded his subjects and then asked them to walk for an hour in a straight line. Without exception, people couldn't do it. Of course everybody thought they were walking in a straight line, until they removed the blindfolds and saw their crooked path. As Krulwich observes,

> This tendency has been studied now, for at least a century. On npr.org we animated field tests from the 1920s, so you can literally see what happens to men who are blindfolded and told to walk across a field in a straight line, or swim across a lake in a straight line . . . and they couldn't. In the animation, you see them going into these strange loop-de loops in either direction. Apparently, there's a profound inability in humans to go straight.[2]

According to this research, there's only one way we can walk in a straight line: by focusing on something ahead of us—like a building, a landmark, or a mountain. If we can fix our eyes on something ahead of us, we can make ourselves avoid our normal, crooked course. Krulwich concludes, "Without external cues, there's apparently something in us that makes us turn [from a straight path]."

I'll tell you what: That's pretty good advice this Advent. If you want to walk in a straight line, then stop focusing on yourself, stop looking at the ground, and by all means don't turn around, look at where you've come from, and try to walk backwards. The only way to walk in a straight line is to focus on the One who is ahead of you. If you can fix your eyes on Jesus, then you can avoid the crooked course and keep from turning away from God.

* * * *

No wonder Mark begins with the words of John the Baptist. His words burst onto the scene like flashing lights in our rearview mirror, to tell us that we are going too fast, veering from side to side, and that if we don't change the way we are moving, we are going to cause ourselves and others great harm.

The only thing to do is to wake up and be prepared. *Doubly* prepared. We need to do the inner work that is necessary to change our hearts, confess our sins, seek God's forgiveness, and become the very vessels that can receive the message of hope and love that God wishes to reveal to us in Jesus. And being prepared means living in anticipation of holy moments that are, in fact, available to us through the bread and the cup, as well as the waters of baptism.

It means living a sacrificial and sacramental life, in which we become the very bread that Jesus takes, blesses, breaks, and gives out for the world, so that we can become the very incarnation of the Incarnate One among us.

I don't know about you, but this holiday season is usually a crazy, busy time for me. We get so caught up in checking off our Christmas gift lists, attending and hosting parties, and being so caught up in the merriment of the season, that we forget the best and most effective way of preparing for Christmas starts first with what is in our hearts. It means setting our hearts straight and asking God to reveal to us everything that is wayward in our lives.

That is the central message of Mark's opening to his Gospel. No angels, no shepherds, no mention of Mary and Joseph, nothing we would expect to find in any Christmas play or cantata. Instead, there is a voice crying out in the wilderness. "Prepare the way for the Lord; make his paths straight."

It may not sound like much of a Christmas, but it sure sounds a whole lot like Advent.

Reflection Questions:

1. When have you ever been lost and needed to consult a guide to find your direction? Or when have you ever been pulled over for speeding and needed to slow down? In the aftermath of those experiences, how did your perspectives and behavior change?

2. How do you need to slow down and pay more attention to your own spiritual preparations during Advent? What are the items on your holiday to-do list that might get in the way?

Digging Deeper:

1. Remembrance, in the sacramental sense, is not just recalling the past; it is dynamically reliving it in the present, and anticipating it in the future. What difference does this idea make in your understanding of baptism and Communion?

2. Can you think of other things that you remember or anticipate in this way? What are they, and how is this type of remembering different than your normal recollection?

3. What parts of your life need to be "made straight" today? What do you need to focus on in order not to "deviate to the right or to the left"?

Awaiting the Already:

Consider taking on a spiritual discipline during Advent this year. You might choose to spend several minutes in silent prayer every day, or develop a daily pattern of reading the Scriptures, or determine to do a regular act of service or generosity. Whatever you choose, write it down and put it in a prominent place to help you remember to do it regularly. You may even wish to set a daily reminder on your phone. How will this discipline help you to "make straight" the imminent work of Christ in your life?

Prayer:

God of power and love, thank you for the life and work of John the Baptist, who calls us even today to slow down, pay attention, and prepare for the coming of Christ. Help us to live sacramentally, to experience the grace of God in every moment. Amen.

---

1. From "A Service of Word and Table I," in *The United Methodist Hymnal*; page 10.
2. From "A Mystery: Why Can't We Walk Straight?" by Robert Krulwich for NPR News Morning Edition (11-22-10). *http://www.npr.org/blogs/krulwich/2011/06/01/131050832/a-mystery-why-can-t-we-walk-straight*. Accessed 8 April 2015.

MATTHEW

Joseph and Herod
"The World As It Is"

READ: MATTHEW 1:1—2:18

B y the second week in Advent, the commercial Christmas cultural machine is in full gear. Shopping malls are filled to the brim with shoppers listening to "It's the Most Wonderful Time of the Year" over the public address speakers. Radio stations are playing nostalgic ditties like "Have Yourself a Merry Little Christmas." And before too long, television screens will begin playing the first of many repetitions of the Frank Capra classic, *It's a Wonderful Life*.

In other words, the culture around us would want you to believe that the world, for a moment, has put its normal regularly scheduled programming on hold and replaced it with a massive in-breaking of good cheer, peaceful tidings, and remarkable joy. Forget Disney World trying to be the "Happiest Place on Earth." Commercial advertisers want you to believe that the earth has its Happiest Time at Christmas.

But you and I know better, don't we? First of all, we know that Christmas hasn't technically arrived yet, so any inclination we have to wish people a "Merry Christmas" is

31

premature according to the church calendar. We aren't at
Christmas yet; we are in Advent. Besides, for many people,
there is very little that makes this world exactly *merry*.
Wars, brokenness, violence, oppression, heartache, grief,
and betrayal do not magically disappear in early December.
There is too much darkness in this world simply to gloss over
it and pretend it is not there, all for the sake of secularized
merriment and plastic good cheer.

It is over and against this romanticized portrait of Christmas
that Matthew brings us an Advent narrative more in keeping
with reality. Forget bright lights, inflatable Nativity figures, and
cheery Christmas cards: Matthew's birth story seems to leap
straight off the headlines from the front-page news.

One of the first people we meet is Joseph, who is greeted
by the traumatizing news that his fiancée, Mary, is now
pregnant with a child that is not biologically his. He receives
the announcement of Jesus' birth not with cheer and gladness,
but with shock and sober deliberation.

Then there is Herod, a villain if there ever was one in the
New Testament. He encounters the news of Jesus' arrival with
abject paranoia, rivaling only his lust for power and sheer
determination to defeat this threat to his throne with violence.

We also see the magi, who aren't technically a part of the
Christmas story; they are more for the time of Epiphany, after
Christmas. But their mention in the Gospel of Matthew (the
only Gospel in which they appear) underscores the kind of
tension that fills Matthew with its characteristic drama.

And all of these people are preceded by a lengthy, and often
overlooked, introduction to the Gospel: Matthew's genealogy,
the ancestral tree of Jesus.

Let's take a look at these pieces one at a time and see
together how Matthew prepares us for a Jesus that is already
here, by portraying the world as it really is.

Joseph

If *TMZ* or *Entertainment Tonight* were around in first-century Palestine, they would have been all over a story brewing in the little town called Bethlehem. News of a young woman becoming pregnant out of wedlock had instant scandal written all over it, the kind of tabloid fodder that goes viral through gossip grapevines and rumor mills.

For what it's worth, we don't see Mary's side in Matthew. It's up to Luke to give us her story in detail. Instead, Matthew provides us with Joseph's point of view, revealing his perspective through a sympathetic lens. He is called a "righteous man" (Matthew 1:19), which immediately conjures up images of Noah, Job, and others throughout the Bible who were beset with suffering despite doing and saying all the right things. He is the embodiment of some of the most challenging stories in the Old Testament, as we cannot help but ask the question on his behalf: "Why do bad things happen to good people?"

When we consider the world as it really is, we recognize that sometimes the righteous do, in fact, suffer. There is nothing about our allegiance to God that makes us immune to heartache and disappointment. Despite our best efforts to stay on the straight and narrow, as we saw Mark prescribe in the previous chapter, we are still subject to the forces of injustice and oppression that seem to prevail in our time.

So notice what the angel says to Joseph at the very beginning of the dream. He does not say to this righteous man, "Don't worry, your problem is solved." Or "Good news! Things are going to get better!" And certainly not, "Buck up, Joseph, it's the first Christmas! It's the most wonderful time of the year!"

No, instead it is a simple but powerful message: "Don't be afraid . . ." (Matthew 1:20). It is a word of frank challenge rather than false hope. It is, on the one hand, an acknowledgment of all that has happened to Joseph and Mary, a recognition that fear is an understandable response. But it is also a call to resistance, and a refusal to let the trauma of external circumstances consume Joseph with fear and disillusionment.

If awaiting the already in Matthew first means acknowledging the reality of a broken world, it also means refusing to live in fear.

Why? Because right after the angel's pep talk, there is a promise: "She will give birth to a son, and you will call him Jesus, because he will save his people from their sins" (Matthew 1:21).

What's remarkable about these words is that the angel provides no proof that what he says is true. There is no hard evidence that the baby comes from the Holy Spirit, rather than another man, as the angel tells Joseph (Matthew 1:20). The angel conducts no pregnancy test, no sonogram, no blood test to prove fatherhood. Instead of proof, there is a promise. Carry through with this pregnancy and keep this family together, and this child will be the Savior of the world.

Joseph, noble and righteous Joseph, has a choice: Take the angel at his word and do the difficult thing, or buckle to the pressures of prevailing culture and do what is expedient. He can preserve Mary's life and put his own reputation on the line, or save his hide and put Mary away.

We all know what Joseph chooses, of course. But Matthew would not want us to skip ahead to the conclusion without pondering for a moment the complexity of his choice. It would be similar to the kind of decision the magi would have to make later in Matthew Chapter 2. In a world that is so broken, where we are tempted to bend toward the culture, do we choose God's way or the easy way?

Just like John the Baptist sets the tone of alertness and sobriety at the beginning of Mark, the man Joseph introduces one of the central themes of Matthew: We must choose to follow Jesus, especially when it is costly to do so. We must stay focused on the daily choices, the everyday challenges, that have at stake our allegiance to Christ.

Herod

Every good story needs a villain, an antagonist who helps to create the tension that gives a narrative its pulse. In Matthew, King Herod fulfills that role like no other. And of all the Gospel writers to record the villainous Herod the Great, it makes sense that it would be Matthew.

In fact, it would not be too much of a stretch to suggest that Matthew's depiction of Herod closely parallels the Old Testament portrait of Pharaoh in Exodus 1–15. Both were tyrannical rulers who governed with a heavy hand and a paranoid mind. The Egyptian ruler Pharaoh interpreted the Israelite population as a threat to his people and his power (Exodus 1:9-10), just as Herod received word of the birth of a new baby king (Matthew 2:3). Both ordered the massacre of innocent children as an extreme measure to eradicate that threat. Moses escaped when his mother placed him in a basket in the river, and Jesus was taken to safety (ironically) in Egypt with his family (Exodus 1:15–2:10; Matthew 2:13-18).

As striking as these parallels with Pharaoh are, history paints an even darker picture of Herod the Great than we find in Matthew. He was so protective of his power that he came to see his own sons as a threat. Eventually he had three of them executed, in addition to his grandfather-in-law and one of his wives. There was a saying back in those days, attributed to Augustus, that "it's better to be Herod's pig than his son" (Macrobius, Saturnalia, 2.4.11). The joke was that as a Jew Herod didn't eat pork, so pigs were safe around him while his own children were not.

Herod also made hollow appeals to the Jews. Even though he was a Jew himself, his loyalties were primarily to Rome and always to himself. He promised to renovate the Jews' beloved Temple and began an impressive rebuilding project that could have rivaled Pharoah's great pyramids. He imported the gold and the wood and remade the Temple with unprecedented glory. But Herod had ulterior plans, seeking to build up his own reputation and curry favor with Rome. He built an impressive palace and other Greco-Roman buildings in Jerusalem as well as fortresses throughout Judea. Even as he built up the Temple where Jews worshiped God, Herod also built up himself, establishing and securing his throne and his power.

And so with a narrative in need of a villain, Matthew serves up one of history's worst in Herod the Great. It is compelling to note that with all the favorite characters we associate with the birth of Jesus—Mary, shepherds, angels, Elizabeth, Zechariah—Matthew focuses on only the magi, Joseph, and Herod.

In many ways, Matthew sets up a dichotomy between an obedient Joseph and a defiant Herod, which sums up the two possible responses to God. And in Matthew, it is a choice given in the context of fear. Fear was the prevailing force in the world at the time of Jesus' birth. For Joseph, it was fear of scandal, trauma, and repercussion. Mary's pregnancy threatened not only her well-being, but also Joseph's own affairs, as well as the very fabric of an ordered, law-abiding society. For Herod, there was a paranoid fear of losing control over his power and authority, along with his ability to direct his own destiny.

Indeed, the backdrop of Matthew is one littered with fearful, menacing forces, all threatening to life. And while Matthew invites us to consider the connection between Herod and Pharoah, the ancient enemy of God's people, it is permissible also to think about the gloomy world Matthew portrays and its similarities to our own. Matthew would not want us to use the imminent arrival of Jesus to escape from the miseries of this world, but to confront them squarely in the face.

In fact, Matthew would not only discourage us from finding Jesus apart from our world, or apart from our time; he would invite us to find the presence of Jesus right in the midst of this world, right now.

Jesus Is Already Here

Consider two of the stories that find themselves only in Matthew's Gospel. The first is the parable of the sheep and the goats in Matthew 25:31-46. The second is Jesus' final instructions to his disciples in Matthew 28:18-20.

In the parable of the sheep and the goats, we see the rule of a heavenly king whose reign extends until the end of time. At the final judgment, the king separates people into two groups, the sheep and the goats, based solely on whether or not they cared for the king while he was still on earth.

"Lord, when did we see you," both groups will ask, "hungry . . . thirsty . . . a stranger . . . naked . . . sick . . . or in prison?" (Matthew 25:37-39, 44). The king's response to both groups is that when they did or did not help "the least of these," they helped or did not help the king himself (Matthew 25:40, 45).

Preachers often interpret this passage for its social justice implications, and for good reason. Care for those who have been marginalized, oppressed, and battered by the traumatic experiences of life is to be a central concern to the people of God. The Sermon on the Mount, the most famous collection of teachings Jesus ever uttered in one place, is found in Matthew (with a slightly different version in Luke). It is here that Jesus talks about the poor in spirit, the meek, the persecuted—all those who are too easily pushed to the fringe of society—who are squarely in line to receive the blessings of the kingdom of heaven (Matthew 5–7).

Over and over again, Jesus paid attention to the people that the rest of society was ignoring, and it is incumbent upon us to do the same. To be sheep, rather than goats, we must care for the hungry, the thirsty, the foreigner, the sick, the naked, and the imprisoned.

But the meaning of the parable goes beyond social justice; it shows us how we can find Jesus among us right here and right now. Jesus is present, the parable tells us, in "the least of these." That was a powerful message for Matthew's readers. The Gospel's earliest audience, like many first-century Christians, were eagerly anticipating the second coming of Jesus. It would not be unlike many today who await the imminent return of Jesus. But as the days, months, and years drifted by, the early Christians were beginning to wonder if Jesus was ever going to come back.

It is to these people that Matthew has a unique answer among the four Gospels, which directly answers the central question of this Bible study: If you are waiting for Jesus to come back some day, then stop waiting. You can find him right here on earth, right now, at this very moment. All you have to do is look into the eyes of the marginalized and the oppressed. And when you see their faces, you are looking at the very face of Jesus himself. "To love another person," said Victor Hugo in *Les Miserables*, "is to see the face of God."

The technical theological term for this idea is *realized eschatology*, which means that the eschaton, or the "end times," are actually realized, or evident in the present moment. Of the four Gospels, Matthew reinforced this idea the most. And that brings us to the second story that is unique to Matthew's Gospel: the Great Commission, Jesus' final words to his disciples in Matthew 28:18-20.

Often we think of Matthew 28:18-20 as a commandment for evangelism and missions: "Therefore, go and make disciples of all nations, baptizing them in the name of the Father and of the Son and of the Holy Spirit, teaching them to obey everything that I've commanded you" (Matthew 28:19-20). Clearly there is a call to witnessing and sharing the good news throughout the world. And notice again the call to live into the sacrament of baptism, which we read about in Mark.

But the passage goes on, and the very last words of the Gospel underscore Matthew's realized eschatology: "Look, I myself will be with you every day until the end of this present age."

There is no mistaking what Jesus is saying here. His departure at the time of the Ascension did not create an absence. He is always with us, every single day, and he will be until the end of time. Once again, if you are waiting for some moment in the future to get to see Jesus face to face, then stop waiting.

Jesus is already here.

And that brings us all the way back to the beginning of Matthew's Gospel, where he alone gives us the very name we most closely associate with Jesus during the season of Advent. It comes in the story of Joseph, where Matthew quotes a prophecy from Isaiah that a virgin will become pregnant and give birth to a son named *Emmanuel* (Matthew 1:23).

Why Emmanuel, and why here in the Book of Matthew? Well, it makes perfect sense. *Emmanuel* means, "God is with us." And that's a message Matthew would want his readers to remember, over and over again in his Gospel.

Genealogy

But let's not forget one more curious aspect of Matthew's birth narrative. In addition to Herod and Joseph, Matthew begins his Gospel with the rather lengthy—and often overlooked—ancestral tree (Matthew 1:1-17).

Luke has a genealogy in his Gospel too (Luke 3:23-38), but Matthew's version is both unique and consistent with the themes we have discovered in this chapter so far.

Matthew's genealogy of Jesus is based on the number seven. In the ancient world, and in the mindset of the Jews, numbers had important meaning. And among the most important numbers was the number seven. Seven, we remember, was the number of days in the week, and the seventh day of the week was the Sabbath, the day of rest, wholeness, and healing. It was the day that creation was completed.

So whenever the number seven occurs in the Bible, it suggests wholeness and completeness and, by extension, restoration and healing.

When the Peter asks Jesus, "Lord, how many times should I forgive my brother or sister who sins against me? Should I forgive as many as seven times?" Jesus answers, "Not just seven times, but rather as many as seventy-seven times" (Matthew 18:21-22). Jesus is not choosing a random large number, as if to tell Peter that he must forgive "a lot." Forgiveness, according to Jesus, is a participation in the grand, cosmic effort by God to restore and reconcile creation back to its created order. It is no coincidence that this conversation is recorded in the Gospel of Matthew.

So, here we have Matthew's Gospel beginning with the reminder that Jesus came into the world following three sets of fourteen generations, forty-two total generations of people from Abraham to Jesus. Forty-two, of course, is six times seven—six sets of seven generations. And that means that when Jesus was born, he ushered in the seventh set of seven generations. He is the ultimate completer of completion, the great restorer of restoration. His arrival signifies the greatest and final work of God to bring healing and wholeness to this broken, bruised, and conflicted world.

To remind us of that fact, Matthew sprinkles into his genealogy a motley crew of some of the most unlikely characters you would expect to see in the ancestry of the Messiah. Rahab is mentioned there (verse 5): a prostitute whom God used to save the spies before Joshua invaded Canaan (see Joshua 2:1-21). David is mentioned there (verse 6): the adulterer and killer who would be Israel's greatest king. And Rehoboam is mentioned there (verse 7): David's grandson, a foolish ruler whose poorly informed policies led to the division of his kingdom (see 1 Kings 12.1-24).

You see, Matthew is not interested in scrubbing and polishing Jesus' ancestors in order to make them look good for the family portrait. Instead, he wants to remind us that even Jesus' ancestors were themselves evidence of how broken and sinful this world had become, and why Jesus' arrival was all the more necessary.

In other words, when Emmanuel arrived, God not only came to be with us. God came at just the right time.

Living in the Present

Put all of these elements together—a realistic portrait of a world filled with fear, the guarantee of Christ's presence right now, and the promise of God's constant, faithful work to restore and heal us—and do you know what you get? Not only do you get an accurate summary of the key features of Matthew's birth narrative, you also get some solid footing to live your life without fear in the midst of troubling times.

Life, after all, is filled with constant vacillations between hilltops and valleys, highs and lows. We chart our time with linear progressions of days and years, but life is never a straight line forward. It is an undulating wave, meandering through triumphs and tragedies at a random pace, surprising us around every bend with what lies next. There is no predictability to life, no surefire way of foreseeing the future. We yearn for what lies ahead, only to realize that it cannot surely be grasped. We cast anchor for the past, back to the "good old days," fickly forgetting that the nature of change makes such a return impossible.

All we have with any certainty is the here and now. Our only true task is not to fret about tomorrow or get stuck in yesterday, but to focus on the gift of the present moment. The more we live into and breathe through every moment as it comes, the more we realize that our lives are actually never static, nor our existence ever still. There is movement in every moment.

Ultimately, here is what Matthew's birth narrative tells us: No matter what you are going through, God is in it. Your life may be a lot like Joseph's right now, and the pain of your struggle may be so intense that you cannot see through the fog of your disillusionment to sense anything beyond the trauma. But there is a redemptive hand already at work. God is at work in the midst of uncertainty, because God lives in the ambiguities. That's how a mysterious God operates: just beyond the reach of our senses and sensibilities, but fully approachable through our faith. "He who learns must suffer," said the Greek playwright Aeschylus. "And even in our sleep pain that cannot forget falls drop by drop upon the heart, and in our own despite, against our will, comes wisdom to us by the awful grace of God."[1]

Even if life for you is calm and serene, watch out: God is at work. You may not see your own comparisons to the life of Herod, but they may be there. As long as there is an inkling within us that flirts with the fallacy that we are self-made creatures, and as long as we walk with a puffy-chested, thumb-nosing swagger, God is ready to conform us into a likeness of humble service that fulfills the image of God within us. It's not to say that God causes trauma to teach us a lesson. I don't believe in that. But it is to say that when life is going well, sin exerts its greatest influence, as pride, gluttony, and laziness impede the way of holy living.

May you experience that "awful grace of God" in the midst of your lives, in every present moment. May you come to know the joy that comes in trusting God in the midst of your hardship, as you take your journey through the ups and downs of life, one step at a time.

And remember: Emmanuel. God is with us.

Reflection Questions:

1. What is your overall mood during Advent so far? Is it good cheer and excitement, worry over hardships and suffering, or something in between?

2. Matthew paints a realistic picture of the difficult world into which Jesus was born. Is there anything freeing about allowing yourself to do the same? What painful realities do you call to mind at this time of year?

3. Have you ever studied in detail your own family tree? What have you discovered about yourself as you have learned about your ancestors?

Digging Deeper:

1. Matthew places the stories of Joseph and Herod side by side to illustrate contrasting responses to the disrupting news of the arrival of Jesus. How would you characterize the responses of Joseph and Herod? What similarities and differences do you find between them?

2. In what way is the Advent anticipation for Jesus disruptive for you? How do you respond to it? Do you liken your response more to Herod or to Joseph?

3. What difference does it make to your anticipation of Jesus' return to know that Matthew advocates for a Jesus who is already here? How does that change the way you live in the present moment and relate to people in need?

Awaiting the Already:

While the parable of the sheep and goats (Matthew 25:31-46) is not technically part of the birth narrative, it can still be read in the context of Advent as people await the return of Jesus. Consider those around you who are hungry, thirsty, lonely, sick, or imprisoned. Research or discuss a way that you can reach out to them through your church or a community program. This week, serve those whom you identify. Recognize that in "the least of these," you are face to face with Christ who is already here.

Prayer:

God, we thank you for your constant presence among us, and for the way in which we can find Jesus among the least, the last, and the lost. Empower us to minister to those in need, that we might see Jesus among us. Amen.

---

1. Aeschylus, *Agamemnon* I.179. Quoted in *The Greek Way*, by Edith Hamilton (Norton, 1964); page 194.

LUKE

Zechariah, Elizabeth, Mary, and the Shepherds "The Ultimate Advent Playlist"

READ: LUKE 1:5—2:20

Not that I'm advocating partiality, but I suspect that Luke is our favorite Advent Gospel. It's the one that contains the stories we most often associate with the season. It has the poignant relationship between Elizabeth and Mary. It has the beautiful words of Mary's song, the Magnificat. And it has the story we most often hear on Christmas Eve: the shepherds' visit by the angels and the joyful announcement of Jesus' birth. (Even Linus van Pelt memorized it for the *Peanuts* Christmas special!) It is quite likely that if you want to find a part of the Christmas story in the Bible, your best bet is to start with Luke.

Luke is also unique in the manner of writing he brings to the Christmas story. Mark wrote with urgency and a sparse narrative style, and Matthew wrote with an ominous tone. John (we will discover) wrote with poetic flourish. But Luke wrote with a song in his head. There's no other way to explain why nearly every major character in Luke's Nativity story breaks out into a song at some point. Luke is

47

a lot like a Rodgers and Hammerstein musical: Something happens to someone, and then they sing about it. So if Mark is like a *Reader's Digest*, Matthew is like a Steven King novel, and John is like a Shakespeare play, then Luke is like a Broadway musical.

Luke really loves his songs. And come to think of it, isn't that true of all of us?

The Power of Songs

What music gives you chills? Are there pieces of music that often manage to give you goose bumps when you hear them? I think of Puccini's "Nessun Dorma," and its exhilarating, swelling crescendos. Morten Lauridsen's "O Magnum Mysterium" evokes images of God's grandeur and majesty. And nothing quite beats a chancel choir singing Handel's "Hallelujah Chorus." These and many other selections never fail to give me the shivers.

As it turns out, music-induced chills are scientifically measurable phenomena. A recent study published in the journal *Social Psychology and Personality Science* revealed that certain songs can trigger activity in a person's hypothalamus, the part of the brain responsible for hunger, rage, and involuntary responses like blushing and goose bumps.[1]

But here's the interesting part: The researchers found that the style or genre of music did not determine these responses. What's more important is what they termed a person's "openness to experience," one's willingness to be moved by the music (as well as other aesthetic and artistic experiences).

Now, I'm pretty sure that Luke the Gospel writer knew nothing about brain anatomy and personality science. But he sure knew a lot about emotive music: Every time something great happens to someone, they break into song. Consider Mary's Magnificat, or Zechariah's prophecy, or Elizabeth's song in seclusion. Though Luke's biblical text tells us that the people "said" these things, the poetic nature of their expression and speech is more consistent with song, like what we find in the Psalms. And often, those songs emerge from a person's deep well of emotion, accompanied by great joy and awe bordering on fear. More than their counterparts in Matthew, Luke's angels are always telling people not to be afraid (Luke 1:13, 30; 2:10).

Apparently, there are plenty of goose bumps to go around in Luke.

We might say that Luke's Gospel is written for people who are particularly "open to experience"—open to the possibility of a surprising word of good news, open to a new song that will overwhelm cacophony and chaos, and open to the arrival of a God who brings harmony in the midst of dissonance.

How about you? Will you be open to the soul-stirring sounds of Christmas and allow its music to give you shivers? Will you deafen the drones of deadlines and to-do lists, and listen for the overwhelming hush of a faint baby's cry and the glorious songs of angels in the sky? Will you quiet the noise within your soul and raise your antenna heavenward?

Zechariah: A Song From Silence

Let's take each of these songs one at a time, beginning with Zechariah and Elizabeth in Luke Chapter 1.

Zechariah was an elderly priest who lived under the rule of King Herod. He and his wife Elizabeth were quite elderly and childless, despite their most earnest prayers. One day, as he was in the Temple performing his priestly work, the angel Gabriel came to him, terrifying Zechariah, and saying:

> Don't be afraid, Zechariah. Your prayers have been heard. Your wife Elizabeth will give birth to your son and you must name him John. He will be a joy and delight to you, and many people will rejoice at his birth, for he will be great in the Lord's eyes. . . . He will bring many Israelites back to the Lord their God. He will go forth before the Lord, equipped with the spirit and power of Elijah. . . . He will make ready a people prepared for the Lord (Luke 1:13-17).

Wow. Talk about good news! You would think this would have given Zechariah reason to rejoice. If this were a word association game, we would assume that Zechariah's next words would have been, "Hallelujah," or "Amen," or "Thank You."

Nope. Instead, Zechariah asks, "How can I be sure of this? My wife and I are very old" (verse 18). To paraphrase, what Zechariah meant was: "You've got to be kidding me. Are you nuts? Do you see this face? Do you know how old I am? Do you know how old my wife is? And how do you suggest we raise this child? I may be dead and gone by the time the kid reaches puberty!"

Before we criticize Zechariah too harshly, let's just be honest here. Isn't his reaction similar to the kind of disbelief and skepticism we display once December rolls around and we prepare for Christmas? How many of us, even in the last few days, have thought or uttered something like:

"Peace on Earth? You've got to be kidding. There's nothing like that nowadays."

"This is a season of hope? I can barely keep my life together right now!"

"Joy and gladness? For me? How is this possible?"

It's true. In the midst of all this chaos and frustration, when the good news of Jesus comes to us, we can hardly believe it. It all seems too extraordinary, too wild, and too far-fetched to believe. So, like Zechariah, we say, "How will I know that this is so? How could this be?"

To which the angel responded: "I am Gabriel. I stand in God's presence. I was sent to speak to you and to bring this good news to you. . . . But because you didn't believe, you will remain silent, unable to speak until the day when these things happen" (Luke 1:19-20).

Suddenly, the priest Zechariah lost his voice. Now I don't know about you, but I could hardly imagine a worse fate for a clergy person. A preacher who couldn't talk? It would be like a chef who couldn't taste or a taxi driver who couldn't see. It all sounds pretty inconvenient for poor Zechariah.

But something happened to Zechariah over the next nine months. In the quiet of his own mind, he had time to reflect and think. Perhaps he was put on leave from his regular priestly duties. Maybe he spent more time at home, away from Jerusalem. Maybe he had lots of opportunities to imagine his life with a little boy to call his own. Perhaps he watched his wife's belly get bigger and bigger and noticed his deepest anxieties grow smaller and smaller.

It turns out that the silence from the angel was not a curse after all, but a remedy.

After the child was born, a disagreement arose over what the child's name should be (Luke 1:57-61). Some said he should be called "Zack, Jr.," while Elizabeth wanted to name him John. But a still mute Zechariah picked up a writing tablet and wrote the words, "His name is John," just as the angel had told him (verse 63).

At that moment, his throat tickled and his tongue wiggled, and the vocal chords that had been atrophying into nothing burst into new, purposeful life. And Luke records an amazing song of praise that Zechariah offered to God, in gratitude for the amazing gift of his son and acknowledging the impact he will make on the world (Luke 1:67-79). Just consider these words from Zechariah's song (verses 76-79):

> "You, child, will be called a prophet of the Most High,
>   for you will go before the Lord to prepare his way.
> You will tell his people how to be saved
>   through the forgiveness of their sins.
> Because of our God's deep compassion,
>   the dawn from heaven will break upon us,
>   to give light to those who are sitting in darkness
>   and in the shadow of death,
>   to guide us on the path of peace."

Now, do you think there was any way for Zechariah to have come to this conclusion were it not for the silence he endured? Do you think there is a lesson to be learned from this man who was at first much too distracted by his present reality to believe something that ultimately could change his life?

You bet there is.

Silence is a teacher, and it conveys a lesson we must all take to heart, especially at this time of the year. How much do you really have to do in this time leading up to Christmas? How about this: What if you were as intentional in creating moments of stillness and silence as you are in crossing items off your Christmas to-do lists? It would seem impossible at first. After all, there are presents to buy, parties to throw, events to attend, houses to decorate, preparations to make, costumes to sew, food to cook, calls to make, cards to mail. . . . And then the angel said, "I was sent to speak to you and to bring this good news to you . . . But because you didn't believe, you will remain silent, unable to speak until the day when these things happen . . ."

Isn't it time you unplugged all the Christmas noise? Wouldn't it really be okay if you attended one less party this year? Wouldn't it be fine if you gave someone a card for Christmas with a thoughtful message rather than an expensive present? Wouldn't it be nice for you to boycott Christmas commercials and newspaper ads? And wouldn't the glow that comes from experiencing God's hope and love shine more brightly than even the most lavishly decorated tree?

Mary: A Song of Obedience

The second track on Luke's Advent playlist is probably the most famous song in the entire New Testament. It is sung by the artist most often associated with the birth of Jesus, his own mother Mary.

When we meet her, we know little about her except that she is a young girl, engaged to Joseph (Luke 1:27). Later we find out she is a relative of Elizabeth (the Greek term for *relative* doesn't specifically say what the exact family relationship is), which gives us our first indication that the songs of Mary and Zechariah are somehow going to be linked (Luke 1:36).

But notice that it almost wasn't that way. Consider that when the same angel (Gabriel) gave essentially the same news (you're going to be a parent) to both Zechariah and Mary, they responded in virtually the same way: incredulity.

Zechariah: "How can I be sure of this? My wife and I are very old" (Luke 1:18).

Mary: "How will this happen since I haven't had sexual relations with a man?" (Luke 1:34).

The former balked at the news because he was too old. The latter did the same because she was too young. The responses were different for reasons of age and circumstance, but they were equally skeptical.

So why was it necessary for the angel to surprise Zechariah with silence, but not Mary? We can't know for sure. Perhaps Mary received a little more grace because she was young, while Zechariah was a seasoned priest schooled in holy things. Or maybe it was due to the more dangerous position Mary would be in as an unwed pregnant woman. The potential for scandal and even danger for Mary might have caused Gabriel to treat her with more understanding.

Whatever the reason, the angel seems to have given Mary a second chance. First, Gabriel tried to offer an explanation that was a tad more theological than biological: "The Holy Spirit will come over you and the power of the Most High will overshadow you" (Luke 1:35). Not the stuff from your average junior high health class, to be sure. And perhaps Mary was still unconvinced.

So then, the messenger of God went a step further and offered proof, a sign to which Mary could look for reassurance. Mary received proof in the form of her very own relative Elizabeth. "Look, even in her old age, your relative Elizabeth has conceived a son. This woman who was labeled 'unable to conceive' is now six months pregnant. Nothing is impossible for God" (Luke 1:36-37).

And it must have been that last statement that tipped Mary's scale from doubt to belief, because she then said, "I am the Lord's servant. Let it be with me just as you have said" (Luke 1:38).

I don't know if the angel would have moved on to another girl if Mary had said no. There's no reason to ponder that question for very long. But it is important to note that, given the similarity of initial reactions between Zechariah and Mary, it was the proof provided by Elizabeth's pregnancy that brought Mary the assurance she needed.

In other words, before Mary's pregnancy became a blessing to the world, Elizabeth's pregnancy was a blessing to Mary. Elizabeth's pregnancy moved Mary to a place of steadfast commitment and trust, whether Elizabeth knew it or not.

What's important to know here is that both of these pregnancies illustrate the nature of miracles in the Bible. Whenever something miraculous happens in Scripture, it is rarely ever for the benefit of the recipient alone. When someone in the Bible is blessed, it is so that the recipient can become a blessing for others.

We know very little about Elizabeth's reaction to becoming pregnant. Apart from her brief words that God "has shown his favor to me by removing my disgrace" (Luke 1:25), her whole story is told through the perspective of her disbelieving husband. But we do know that Elizabeth became an incredible source of encouragement to her young relative before she even realized it.

That's why, before we even get to Mary's glorious song in verses 46-55, we see a tender encounter between these two matriarchs of the Advent story. Mary rushed to the Judean city where Zechariah and Elizabeth lived (Luke 1:39). She entered their house, and immediately Elizabeth felt her baby kick inside her (Luke 1:41). And then, so as to cement the role that Elizabeth was playing in Mary's life, she offered Mary powerful words of encouragement: "God has blessed you above all women, and he has blessed the child you carry. . . . Happy is she who believed that the Lord would fulfill the promises he made to her" (Luke 1:42-45).

Just as John the Baptist was a forerunner of Jesus, so it was with their mothers: Elizabeth was a forerunner of Mary. Elizabeth modeled for Mary what it meant to be both a recipient and a conduit of God's miracle. She showed her that when one is blessed by God, one must be a blessing for others. That's what Elizabeth became for Mary, so that Mary could become the same for the whole world.

That, finally, is what set the stage for the most beautiful song in the entire New Testament (Luke 1:46-55). A song that, at first, seems fairly autobiographical:

"With all my heart I glorify the Lord!
    In the depths of who I am I rejoice in God my savior.
He has looked with favor on the low status of his servant.
    Look! From now on, everyone will consider me highly favored
            because the mighty one has done great things for me" (verses 46-49).

But it doesn't take long before there is a major shift in the content and focus of Mary's song. After the first three verses, it becomes less about what God has done for Mary, and more about what God will do through Mary. The vessel has become a conduit:

"Holy is his name.
        He shows mercy to everyone,
        from one generation to the next,
        who honors him as God.
He has shown strength with his arm.
    He has scattered those with arrogant thoughts and proud inclinations.
    He has pulled the powerful down from their thrones
    and lifted up the lowly.

He has filled the hungry with good things
   and sent the rich away empty-handed.
He has come to the aid of his servant Israel,
      remembering his mercy,
      just as he promised to our ancestors,
      to Abraham and to Abraham's descendants forever."
                                              (verses 49-55)

Mary's song is critically important to the Advent story. The season is simply not complete without including it. It is a song with two verses, first about Mary being blessed by God, and then about God using Mary to be a blessing for others.

That is an important theme for Advent pilgrims waiting for a Jesus who is already here. For those of us who have been given the gift of Jesus Christ, we must then bear that gift for others in need. We can be an Elizabeth to the Marys around us, or a Mary to the world around us. We can be that gift of encouragement to others, so that God's blessing can flow through them as well.

Angels: A Song of Joy

And then, of course, we get to the angels and the shepherds. Luke 2:1-20 has become the staple Scripture for Christmas Eve services, and it's hard to read this passage without listening to it with the child-like wonder of Linus van Pelt in *A Charlie Brown Christmas*. For many of us, Luke's Nativity story *is* Christmas. It evokes carols and candle lighting, and memories of cherished holidays past.

To be sure, the angels' song is full of marvel and spectacle. Even the key words of their song pop out like lights in the night sky: *Good News* . . . *Savior* . . . *Glory* . . . *Peace*. But notice how the song starts: "Don't be afraid" (Luke 2:10).

We now see that this phrase is a common theme for all of Luke's songs. For Zechariah, Mary, and now the shepherds, the first utterance of the angels to these Advent characters is a word of comfort in the midst of their fear.

For these shepherds, entrusted with the sole task of caring for their flock, this kind of threat—one that popped out of nowhere and rained down from the night sky—had to be downright terrifying. There was much to fear in that moment. Besides, these were shepherds, not soldiers. They were lowly, humble workers, not people of status or notoriety. There was much about their surrounding society that would make ordinary people fearful.

There was the oppressive reign of the Roman government. There was heavy taxation. There was the forced census. There were generations of being passed around like batons between whatever empire ruled at the time: first the Babylonians, then the Persians, then the Greeks, then the Seleucids, and now the Romans. There were the years, centuries, of longing for freedom and liberation, in anticipation of the Messiah.

It was over against this dark night sky, this canvas of suffering and sadness, that the angelic choir sang a melody that would echo for all eternity: "Glory to God in heaven, and on earth peace among those whom he favors" (Luke 2:14).

Don't you think the world needs to hear a song of hope today? Just ask Vedran Smailovic´.

The Cellist of Sarajevo

The 2008 novel *The Cellist of Sarajevo* is a fictionalized retelling of the horrors of the Bosnian War in the early 1990's, in which the capital city of Sarajevo underwent the longest siege of a capital city in modern warfare.[2] It lasted from 1992 to 1996, during which time nearly 14,000 people were killed and over 100,000 homes and buildings were damaged or destroyed.

In the book, one of those buildings was a bakery, which was bombed by mortar shells in 1992, killing 22 people waiting in line for bread. In the immediate aftermath of the attack, rescue personnel and neighbors rushed to the scene to help the victims, including a thirty-five-year-old gentleman named Vedran Smailovic´.

Smailovic´ was not a doctor, or politician, or soldier. By many standards, he was essentially powerless to address the persistent rain of mortar shells and random sniper fire that deluged his beloved city on a daily basis. Smailovic´ was a musician, an accomplished cellist with the Sarajevo Philharmonic Orchestra.

In the wake of the bombing at his nearby bakery, Smailovic´ did the one thing he knew how to do well. He took his cello to the very site where those twenty-two innocent victims were killed, and he began playing the hauntingly melancholy Adagio in G Minor by Tomaso Albinoni. For twenty-two straight days, one for each of the victims, the cellist played the same song, in various places around Sarajevo where violence and destruction had consumed the city. He often played right in the midst of rubble, or at funerals of the deceased, or even in open courtyards in the dead aim of sniper rifles, as bombs and bullets continued to wreak havoc around him.

His music brought comfort to the grieving and a therapeutic salve to a war-weary country. He provided a real-time soundtrack to the agonies of the suffering, expressing both latent and blatant pain in a way only music

can. But more than that, his public performances embodied
a bold confrontation to the powers at large, proclaiming that
no act of violence, and no evil deed, could thwart the spirit of
a people determined to live in freedom.

****

Perhaps this is why Luke's version of the Christmas story
was written: to provide songs that strengthen the soul in the
midst of suffering. This is the holy task to which God calls
the church. For like the cellist, we have no rightful claim
to political power or military might. The church is neither
politician nor soldier, and history has shown the tragic
consequences whenever the church has tried to assume either
role. Our discipleship demands that our tactics to address
evil must be born of a separate standard and a different ethic,
lest we become the very evil we strive to overcome.

The cellist of Sarajevo might remind us that the church's
calling is one of melodic defiance. Our task is neither to fight
nor to cower, but to sing. It is to claim the songs of peace,
comfort, and courage, daring to perform them where the
world most needs to hear them: not in the shadows or in
the security of safe distances, but directly in the face of the
oppressor, in the line of fire, as a living, lyrical witness to the
power of the Resurrection.

Despite what the secular voices may say, the church is far
from weak, or powerless, or irrelevant. Rather, the church can
offer the very thing that would most remedy a world caught
in an endless cycle of self-destructive behavior: a subversive,
surprising song. A song whose lyrics speak of self-giving love
rather than self-addicted agendas. A song whose sounds are
counter waves to the thrum of war chants and the clanging
of swords. A song whose melody drives us upward towards
holiness and purity, rather than into the darkest recesses of

our sinful instincts. A sacred harmony that pulses with God's unconditional love, calling us to forgiveness.

Yes, it is a dark and broken world. And the temptation might be to cower in fear. But "do not be afraid," the angels sing. For ours is a holy calling. The church has a song to perform, and we each have instruments to play. And God has stepped onto the podium, baton in hand.

Reflection Questions:

1. What do you experience when you hear your favorite, most moving piece of music? How is that sensation different from that which comes from any other sensory experience?

2. What is your favorite song or style of music? What is your favorite Christmas song? What does this song selection suggest about your faith, your personality, and your life in general?

Digging Deeper:

1. Among the key characters in Luke's birth narrative— Zechariah, Elizabeth, Mary, Gabriel, the shepherds, the angels—which do you relate to the most? What spiritual qualities do they have that you would like to embody?

2. How do you resonate with the story of the cellist of Sarajevo discussed above? How does this image inform your understanding of the mission of the church today?

Awaiting the Already:

Take your favorite Christmas song and investigate its meaning and its origins. What is the context in which this song was written? How do these lyrics provide strength to you for your own Advent journey? Read or sing this song each day this week, at a regular time. As you do so, remember the church's calling to play or sing a song of grace and love in our world.

Prayer:

Oh God, who deserves our worship through song and praise, we thank you for giving us the gift of music. May it open our hearts and minds to a fresh in-breaking of the Spirit of Christ, that we might be for the world the melody and lyrics of your love incarnate. Amen.

1. From "'Messiah' give you chills? That's a clue to your personality" for *The Body Odd*, December 10, 2010. *bodyodd.nbcnews.com/_news/2010/12/10/5619731-messiah-give-you-chills-thats-a-clue-to-your-personality.* Accessed 28 April 2015.
2. *The Cellist of Sarajevo*, by Steven Galloway (Riverhead, 2008).

JOHN

The Word Made Flesh
"The Light in the Darkness"

READ: JOHN 1:1-18

F ew passages in the entire New Testament can rival
the poetic artistry and magnificent flourish of the
first eighteen verses of John's Gospel. This passage
simultaneously serves many purposes: It is a prelude to John's
Gospel, a narrative of the Advent of Jesus, and a theological
treatise describing John's Christology, or way of understanding
who Jesus is.

If the Gospel of John were a symphony, the first eighteen verses
would be the opening overture, a grand and majestic beginning
that captures the audience's attention, sparks their imagination,
and introduces the key features of the rest of the composition.

John accomplishes this with words rather than melody,
of course. But these opening verses are nevertheless an
impressive movement, which begins with a wide-angle vision
of the Word's power and prestige and moves to focus in on the
Word Made Flesh.

In other words, these verses transition from majestic to
specific, from telescope to microscope, from the cosmic

preeminent Christ to the finite, incarnate Jesus. One might consider these verses as concentric circles, moving in succession from the grandest down to the smallest:

1. Begin with the widest circle (verses 1-3a), the Word who has existed from the beginning of time, who is the universal creator of all that is: *In the beginning was the Word and the Word was with God and the Word was God. The Word was with God in the beginning. Everything came into being through the Word, and without the Word nothing came into being.*

2. Now zoom in just a tad to the next concentric circle (verses 3b-5), the Word who is the source of all life and light, who vanquishes the darkness: *What came into being through the Word was life, and the life was the light for all people. The light shines in the darkness, and the darkness doesn't extinguish the light.*

3. Then close in on the third circle (verses 9-13), the Word who rules the earth and all its inhabitants: *The true light that shines on all people was coming into the world. The light was in the world, and the world came into being through the light, but the world didn't recognize the light. The light came to his own people, and his own people didn't welcome him. But those who did welcome him, those who believed in his name, he authorized to become God's children, born not from blood nor from human desire or passion, but born from God.*

4. And finally, there is the tightest, most specific circle of all (verse 14), the Word expressed in singular, finite human form in Jesus: *The Word became flesh and made*

his home among us. We have seen his glory, glory like
that of a father's only son, full of grace and truth.

Moving through these concentric circles, John provides
a full and sweeping portrait of the second person of the
Trinity, beginning with his cosmic preeminence and gradually
zooming in to his most visible expression in Jesus of Nazareth.

And just in case this kind of introductory overture sounds
familiar, well, it should. Consider how we've heard a similar
overture during the opening verses of the Old Testament and
the whole Bible, in Genesis 1.

1. Begin with the widest circle (Genesis 1:1-2), the God
   who existed from the beginning, who is the universal
   creator of all that is: *When God began to create the*
   heavens and the earth—the earth was without shape
   or form, it was dark over the deep sea, and God's wind
   swept over the waters.

2. Then, the next circle (Genesis 1:3-5), the God who
   is the source of all light, which God separated from
   the darkness: *God said, "Let there be light." And so*
   light appeared. God saw how good the light was. God
   separated the light from the darkness. God named the
   light Day and the darkness Night.

3. Zoom in a bit (Genesis 1:9-11), and you'll discover
   the God who rules the earth and all its inhabitants:
   God said, "Let the waters under the sky come together
   into one place so that the dry land can appear." And
   that's what happened. God named the dry land Earth,
   and he named the gathered waters Seas. God saw how
   good it was. God said, "Let the earth grow plant life:

plants yielding seeds and fruit trees bearing fruit with seeds inside it, each according to its kind throughout the earth." And that's what happened.

4. God's creation continues (Genesis 1:12-25). Then finally, we reach the most specific circle of all (Genesis 1:26-27), the God whose image is expressed in finite, human form: *Then God said, "Let us make humanity in our image to resemble us so that they may take charge of the fish of the sea, the birds in the sky, the livestock, all the earth, and all the crawling things on earth." God created humanity in God's own image, in the divine image God created them, male and female God created them.*

Clearly, the opening of John's Gospel is intended to offer a compelling parallel to the origins of creation itself, to suggest that what happened in the Incarnation was the inauguration of a new creation and a new covenant through a new divine image in human form, the Word Made Flesh.

If the opening of John's Gospel were an overture, and if one of the features of an overture is the introduction of the entire symphony's key themes, then there is no mistaking what John wishes to be a central facet of his description of Jesus: He is the light in the midst of a dark world. A light so bright that darkness cannot overcome it.

John uses the image of light throughout his Gospel as a way to describe the presence and impact of Jesus in the world.

*   Jesus' famous encounter with Nicodemus in Chapter 3 occurs under the cover of darkness, and Jesus describes those who live in truth as ones who come to the light (John 3:1-21).

- When he teaches in the Temple in Chapter 8, Jesus calls himself the "light of the world." Soon afterward he heals a blind man, removing his darkness and opening his eyes to the light (John 8:12–9:7).
- Prior to raising his friend Lazarus from death and the darkness of the tomb, Jesus challenges his disciples to walk in the light of day to prevent stumbling in the night (John 11:9-10, 38-46).
- After Jesus enters Jerusalem to begin the final week of his life, he calls his followers to believe in the light, so that their lives might be determined by the light (John 12:35-36).

It is no wonder that the prelude to John's Gospel, and the very way he describes Jesus' entry into the world, uses the image of light that has come into darkness, which the darkness cannot overcome.

Darkness and Light

This is good news for people in Advent who are living in darkness, as it is a reminder that sometimes, the light is only visible—and therefore can only be claimed—when one has lived through the darkness of one's life.

On April 17, 1970, the Apollo 13 lunar mission concluded its harrowing six-day space voyage with a safe return to earth. When an oxygen tank exploded two days after launch, the three astronauts on board were forced to deal with limited power, loss of cabin heat, a shortage of water, and a broken carbon dioxide removal system. After aborting their goal of landing on the moon, they attempted a perilous reentry into the earth's atmosphere. They lost radio contact for six minutes during the reentry, with the world waiting in deafening suspense. But finally, to the relief of everyone involved, the men splashed safely into the South Pacific Ocean.

Jim Lovell, the commander of the mission, is rightly praised for his heroism in leading the crew home. He is also credited with uttering one of the most famous phrases in the history of space travel, made more so by the 1995 film *Apollo 13*: "Houston, we have a problem." But this doomed space mission would not be the first time he faced impossible odds in an aircraft while trying to find his way home.

When he was a Navy pilot in the 1950's, Lovell was flying a mission in his F2H Banshee off the coast of Japan. Faulty instruments mistakenly led him away from his aircraft carrier, forcing him to miss his rendezvous point by several miles. Lovell felt hopelessly lost as he flew circles in the dark over the Sea of Japan. As he tried to turn on a cockpit light, his instrument lights suddenly shorted out and everything went black. His chances of survival, let alone a safe return to the aircraft carrier, grew dimmer by the second.

Lovell glanced at the water below, the absence of light both inside and outside the cockpit forcing his eyesight to adjust to the dark. With his vision newly accustomed to the darkness, Lovell was able to spot a faint trail of phosphorescent algae, which had been churned up by the propellers of his crew's aircraft carrier. He followed that glowing trail all the way to a safe landing atop the carrier. Were it not for the darkness that engulfed him from the night sky and his damaged electronics, he would not have spotted the radiant trail that had been present to lead him to safety all along.

"You never know what events are going to transpire to get you home," Lovell said in the movie, which could very well refer to either of his death defying experiences. Indeed, whether it be splashing down to earth from space or landing a fighter jet in a dark sea, Lovell learned that sometimes, one has to go through the darkness in order to recognize and appreciate the light.[1]

Suffering is like the darkness that surrounded Jim Lovell's plane. Just as it forced him to adjust his perception and see a new way forward, your hardship can give you an unexpected chance to recognize a hope that has been with you all along. It does not mean that God wants you to suffer, or that God caused your suffering to begin with. Instead, it reminds us that God is always present to offer us new life, even when we don't recognize it. Sometimes, it takes suffering to help us arrive at that realization.

So let's just acknowledge up front that for many people, and perhaps even for you, this season of light feels a lot more like darkness. Christmas doesn't feel very Christmassy this year. It's not for lack of trying. We see the lights, hear the music, attend the parties, sing the songs, but we don't feel it. Despite our best efforts to practice Christmas, we don't feel Christmas.

It's hard, isn't it? How can one convince you that this is the time for family and friends when you have just buried a loved one and are coping with the loss?

How does one convince you that this is the season for giving and sharing when you've just lost your job, your stock portfolio has plummeted, your business has gone in the tank, or some other crisis has forced you to pare down your Christmas list, wrap fewer presents, and make the stockings a little lighter this year?

How does one convince you that this is the season for peace on earth and goodwill among people when all you see is evidence to the contrary? How does the Christmas message of peace make sense to a war-addicted, revenge-obsessed, violence-propagating culture?

How does one convince you that this is the season for love when all you've seen in your relationships is bitterness, betrayal, mistrust, and resentment?

Consider again those lights that adorn our trees. We will light them, and they will burn brightly and pierce through the darkness. But they also do something else. Notice: When they are obstructed, they create a shadow.

Many Advent pilgrims today have something in common. An obstruction has entered the scene. And just as light creates shadows, the observance of Christmas has created pain surrounding those obstacles. We find ourselves living in the shadowy dark.

With Christmas Day now on the horizon, this is a chance for us to be honest. Times are tough for us, emotionally and otherwise.

The worst thing we can do is try to give each other false hope, plastic good cheer, and shallow encouragement cloaked in friendly advice. All we can do is lift up what John's Gospel makes eminently clear: *What has come into being in Jesus is life, and the life is the light of all people. The light shines in the darkness, and the darkness doesn't extinguish it.*

We might scratch our heads as to the "how" of the Incarnation, but John is more interested in the "why." If we wrestle over exactly how God became human, we miss the point entirely. The point John homes in on is this: God touched the earth in the form of Jesus to save us from our suffering by suffering with us.

Jesus was not born into a world of holiday cheer, festive displays, and widespread goodwill. He entered a world of crowded city streets; inhospitable innkeepers; a paranoid, murderous king; and hopelessly oppressed citizens. As Matthew's Advent reminded us in Chapter 2, Jesus entered the world as it is, with all of its darkness and gloom.

Jesus, too, would learn

- the sting of a loved one's death;
- the heartbreak of a close friend's betrayal;
- the fatigue of keeping up a personal crusade;
- the vengeful backlash that came from simply trying to speak the truth;
- the pain of one day suffering his own torture and death.

Oh, if there is one truth to lift up tonight, one candle to hold up amidst our darkness, it is this:

God has come to be here with you. Not in spite of your suffering, but to share in your suffering. Not in spite of your darkness, but precisely because of it. Because, as the Gospel suggests, you were sitting in darkness, and now you can see a great light.

The Nature of Christ's Light

This is not just any light. This is God's light. And God's light can do something that no other light, natural or fabricated, can claim to do: God's light doesn't create shadows.

It goes against every property of light, every principle of physics I ever learned. Natural light creates shadows when obstructions are in the way. God's light shines through, even when the obstructions of life appear. John's Gospel says it in its poetic, simplistic best.

The light came into the world, and the darkness didn't have a chance.

What kind of light is this? It is not fabricated holiday light, with shopping lists and tinsel wrap. That light creates shadows that only amplify our misery. This light is the light of a God who came near to be with us.

What kind of light is this? It is not the light of unfulfilled hopes and dashed dreams. That light creates shadows and fills us with remorse and bitterness. This light is the light of a God who fills us with the eternal hope of our security in the kingdom of heaven.

What kind of light is this? It is not the light of vengeful war and attacks on our enemies. That light creates permanent shadows and hollow victories. This light is the light of a God who lifts up an irrational vision of peace.

What kind of light is this? It is not the light of fabricated cheer and festive escapism. Those memories will fade, and so will their benefits. This light is the light of a God who says, "Be still, and know that I am God" (Psalm 46:10, NIV).

What kind of light is this? It is the light that says you are not alone. You do not suffer in solitude. You have a companion for your journey. You are joined by One who breathed your air and walked your sod. One who cried your tears, felt your anger, wrestled with your temptations, and felt the sting of saying goodbye.

This companion is Emmanuel. And God is still with us.

For now, that is enough. At this point in your grief, whatever it may be, it is enough to stop here. It is enough to affirm that God has come to identify with your humanity, feel your pain, and accompany the lonely steps along your path.

God is with us—with you—to be a light that shines through your obstructions. God gives you hope that will not fade, peace that will not be understood, love that will not let you go, and joy that will not create shadows.

Reflecting the Light

John's introduction concludes with this reminder of just why the Incarnation is necessary:

No one has ever seen God. God the only Son, who is at the Father's side, has made God known (John 1:18).

The great benefit of the Incarnation is that Jesus reveals the greatness, wonder, and glory of God in a way that we can comprehend. If we were to try to understand the mysteries of God, then it would be like trying to gaze directly at the sun. It would cause us greater harm than benefit. So Jesus came to reflect God's image to us in a way that we could receive it.

Back on October 23, 2014, there was a partial solar eclipse over the country. I have to admit being initially disappointed by it. When I first heard about it, I had eagerly anticipated something more apocalyptic, along the lines of darkness covering Egypt during the days of Moses and Pharaoh (Exodus 10:21-23), or a scene in Mark Twain's novel *A Connecticut Yankee in King Arthur's Court*. But at 4:30, I looked out my living room window and saw nothing but normal daylight. I even went outside to look at the sun directly.

Whoops. That was a mistake.

With my eyes still squinting from sun shock, I drove to the middle school to pick up my daughters. A small crowd had gathered in the parking lot, next to a van from the local museum and planetarium. They had set up a "Solar Eclipse Watch Party" for the public, and I started to walk over to express my condolences. "Bummer of an eclipse," I was prepared to tell them.

But the director of the museum, who was a member of our church, saw me and waved me over. "Want to come take a look?" she asked excitedly. Take a look at what? at a nonevent? I glanced up at the sun to see if anything had changed.

Oops, I did it again.

Partially blinded once more, I stumbled over to their table and noticed they had set up some contraption. It was called a solar scope, a fancy version of the shoebox pinhole reflector that we learned to make as kids. Sunlight entered a small orange tube that protruded through a large cardboard box, then reflected off a convex mirror near the base. The reflected image bounced onto a large display area on the box lid.

There was no mistaking what I was looking at on the display of the solar scope. It was an impressive image of the partial eclipse, perfectly rendered to show even the sunspots in the center of the sun. I could hardly believe what I was looking at. I instinctively glanced up at the sun again, for the third (and thankfully final) time. Then I stared at the reflection and realized details I couldn't possibly capture with my naked eye.

The partial eclipse was happening, after all. I just needed the aid of a reflective device to enjoy it without hurting myself.

When my daughters finally came out of the school, I yelled to them, "Look, girls! It's the partial eclipse! Look up at the sun!"

"Right. Whatever, Dad," my older daughter said. "We're not dumb." They walked straight over to the solar scope and enjoyed the show, proving once again a capacity for common sense that sometimes eludes their old man.

That solar scope functioned for us in the same way that Jesus reflects the light of God for humanity to comprehend. Though God's light is too bright for us to take in directly, we can see it clearly in the incarnate Christ.

But there is an implied invitation here for us as well, and it is the key way for us to await the presence of Christ already among us. We, too, can reflect the light of Christ for others, so that those who walk in darkness can experience the light of God, incarnate in us.

In his biography of Saint Francis, the great theologian and author G. K. Chesterton described the venerable saint as follows:

St. Francis is the mirror of Christ rather as the moon is the mirror of the sun. The moon is much smaller than the sun, but it is also much nearer to us; and being less vivid it is more visible. Exactly in the same sense St. Francis is nearer to us, and being a mere man like ourselves is in that sense more imaginable. Being necessarily less of a mystery, he does not, for us, so much open his mouth in mysteries.[2]

I love Chesterton's description, which applies not just to Saint Francis but to all the saints who have gone before us. They are for us what the moon is to the sun: a glimpse of radiance in a form that we can comprehend. To consider the fullness of God's glory, given our limited and finite capacity, would be like staring directly into the sun. It would offer us little benefit, and it might even cause us harm.

So we turn to the saints, that grand collection of spiritual ancestors whose faithfulness and example pave the way for our own life of faith. Sainthood does not surface regularly in Protestant circles; we often leave it up to our Catholic siblings to talk about canonization and feast days for the saints. But the New Testament makes it clear that those who have finished the course before us comprise a "great cloud of witnesses" that can encourage us with perseverance and faith (Hebrews 12:1).

But we can take it one step further. As Advent pilgrims, we too have the responsibility to reflect that same light for others. We who have already received the light of Christ can share it with others, so that those who live in darkness can see the glory of God.

For those among us who live under the cover of darkness like Nicodemus in John Chapter 3, even in the darkness of shame, sin, guilt, and addiction, we can reflect a light of forgiveness, grace, and acceptance.

For those who are blinded by despair and hopelessness, like the blind man in John Chapter 9, we can offer a light of hope and courage.

For those who live in the shadow of death, like Mary and Martha grieving over Lazarus in John 11, we can embody a light of comfort and a promise of the resurrection.

And for all of us who are awaiting the arrival of the light of Christ once again this Christmas, we can already offer that light to a world that is living in darkness.

Reflection Questions:

1. When have you ever been lost in the dark, either literally or figuratively? How has the experience of darkness taught you to appreciate light in all its forms?

2. Can suffering ever be beneficial? What has your experience been? Think again about the story of pilot and astronaut Jim Lovell. How can darkness be useful in helping us notice the light and be appreciative of it?

Digging Deeper:

1. As opposed to the prose that the other Gospels use to begin their narratives of Jesus, John begins with poetry and artistry. What are the pros and cons of these two genres, in the way they portray Jesus for us? How does John's opening help us see Jesus in a way that the other Gospels do not?

2. Consider again the similarities between the openings of Genesis and John. What difference is there in your understanding of Jesus after seeing the strong comparisons between these two books?

Awaiting the Already:

John says that Jesus is the light, and that light is the life for you and me. In turn, we can be the light of Christ for people in darkness. Think of someone in your life who is experiencing darkness right now. How can you reflect the light of Christ to that person? In the coming days leading up to Christmas, find a way to mirror Christ's love to him or her, so that he or she might receive God's grace.

Prayer:

God, thank you for the light that has come to pierce our darkness. Teach us, then, to be lights of the world that others may be brought into relationship with you. Amen.

1. From *Apollo 13*, by James Lovell and Jeffrey Kluger (Houghton Mifflin Harcourt, 2000); pages 66–71.
2. From *Saint Francis of Assisi*, by G. K. Chesterton (Image, 1987); page 109.

TITUS

"Paul's Christmas Letter"

READ: TITUS 2:11-13

T he weeks leading up to Christmas hardly ever pass by without us receiving at least one Christmas letter from a friend or loved one. Perhaps you even sent one yourself this year. I'm not sure when the tradition started, but some time ago people decided that the simple act of sending a Christmas card was not personal enough. It needed to be accompanied, or even replaced, by a more thorough recollection of all that has happened in a person's or family's life over the past year.

Perhaps it is natural for this kind of year-in-review correspondence to take place around Christmas, as it is so close to the end of the calendar year. It makes sense liturgically as well, since Advent marks the turn of the church's year.

Theologically, the meaning is even more significant. The act of God's Incarnation into the world through Jesus marked a pivotal moment in the history of the world. All events prior to and after it would be evaluated by that singular moment in time when the Word of God became flesh and dwelt among us. As people who are used to experiencing time linearly, the first Christmas provides a unique hinge in our past-present-future.

However, time is not always linear. It often circles around and back to where we have gone before, in anticipation of a future we have already tasted. That is precisely what happens with the Christmas story. We've heard it many times, learned it since our youth, enacted it in our children's Christmas programs, and heard it on countless Christmas Eve services. It is a story whose pages are well worn, whose words echo from prior retellings.

But every time we hear it, it is a different story because we have changed. Much has happened in the twelve months since our last journey to Bethlehem. We have experienced the triumphant highs of life stage celebrations, achievements, rewards, and accomplishments. Our year has been sprinkled with birthday cakes, wedding flowers, diplomas, ribbons, and cheers. But it has also seen its share of sorrows: the somber solace of a graveside, the chilling words of a doctor's diagnosis, the bitter tears of a broken relationship, the dark shadows of guilt over the past, or fear about the future.

Somehow, every time we go back to this same beautiful story of shepherds and angels, Mary and Joseph, Zechariah and Elizabeth, we hear something new. The timeless and loving God is faithful to speak a fresh word over the chaos of our constantly changing lives.

So there is something poignant in reading about the birth of Christ with a Christmas letter in hand. Reminiscing over the lives of your family and friends—and even your own life—in the context of Christmas reminds us that this very thing that God did long ago is still happening today. The reality of the Incarnation is both constant and adaptable, offering a fresh word for today as a hinge between your past and your future.

The (Pastoral) Christmas Letter

It should be no surprise, then, that the lectionary offers a Christmas letter every Christmas Eve. We don't often hear it during worship, since most preachers I know prefer to read the Gospel text from Luke 2 or John 1, or one of the beautiful oracles from Isaiah. That is, after all, what most folks expect to hear on Christmas Eve. When we sing carols and light candles, there is something comforting about hearing of the shepherds and the angels, or the Word who became flesh to dwell among us, or the people who have walked in darkness and have seen a great light.

So, we usually don't read the words of a pastoral letter called Titus, which offers for us the closest thing to a Christmas letter the apostle Paul can give us on Christmas Eve. Titus is part of a group of New Testament letters that also includes 1 and 2 Timothy. Together, these are sometimes called the Pastoral Letters, and their authorship is often attributed to Paul. They provide words of encouragement, instruction, and admonition to the leaders of the early church. Rarely do they tell stories, like the Gospel narratives, or offer poetic artistry like Isaiah and the prophets. Instead, their purpose is to teach and instruct, and so they are a little less popular to hear on Christmas Eve.

But it would be a shame to skip over reading Titus, because tucked among its words is this passage, to which the lectionary draws our attention every Christmas. Take a moment to read this text again, and listen for its meaning in the context of Christmas and our Advent journey together.

Notice how these words not only speak of the past, but also of the future; of Christ's Incarnation, but also his Second Coming:

The grace of God has appeared, bringing salvation to all people. It educates us so that we can live sensible, ethical, and godly lives right now by rejecting ungodly lives and the desires of this world. At the same time we wait for the blessed hope and the glorious appearance of our great God and savior Jesus Christ (Titus 2:11-13).

Observe the verb tenses that bookend those verses. "The grace of God **has appeared**." It begins in the past, celebrating the Incarnation of Christ that has brought salvation to the world. It is the history of our salvation in a six-word summary. That one sentence captures all that God has done prior to and including the arrival of Jesus: the creation of the world; the covenants with Noah, Abraham, Moses, and David; the care for the Israelites in exile; and beyond. And at the very moment Jesus was born into the world, God fulfilled the promise of a redeemer. *The grace of God*—the undeserved, unmerited gift of salvation and redemption for the world— *has appeared*—it is a done deal, unnecessary to be repeated, imitated, or supplemented.

In other words, imagine this as Paul's Christmas letter to the church, much like the ones you've received from family and friends. On it might be a picture of Abraham (here he is, staring up at the stars of the night sky). Somewhere else is a picture of David (strumming on a harp while composing a song). And here is a picture of the Israelites in captivity in Babylon (huddling in sorrow, silently praying for hope). Then, in the middle of this collage of pictures, is a photograph of manger hay, the very fulfillment of every single one of those other pictures.

Paul is saying, "Church, here is your year-in-review." Here is all that God has been busy doing not just in the past twelve

months, but since the beginning of time. You can almost hear
Paul thinking to himself as he writes: "My goodness, God's
been busy!"

But then, notice the change of focus at the end of the
passage: "At the same time *we wait* for the blessed hope and
the glorious appearance of our great God and savior Jesus
Christ." Not all Christmas letters from family and friends
contain a section about "things we are looking forward to in
the upcoming year," but Paul's certainly does. Where he uses
only six words to describe the past, his words flow out one
after another as he describes the future. It's as if he can hardly
contain his anticipation for what he knows still lies ahead.
If you think Jesus coming as a baby was amazing, then wait
until you see *the blessed hope and the glorious appearance of
our great God and savior Jesus Christ.* This letter ends with
a cliff-hanger to end all cliff-hangers. It's almost like Paul is
saying, "Look out, church. You ain't seen nothin' yet."

In this one passage, we have both the past and the future,
embodied in a Jesus who has appeared and will come again.
And this, of course, brings us all the way back to the very
premise of our Advent journey in this book. If there ever was
an Epistle that captured AWAITING THE ALREADY, summarizing
those same inherent tensions that we have discovered in all
four Gospels, it would be this one.

We are awaiting the arrival of a Jesus who is already here.

Awaiting the Already

And how is it that Titus 2:11-13 suggests we await
the already? How is it that we are to live in the present
moment, in the meantime that stands between the
Incarnation and the Second Coming? Well, this passage

makes it pretty clear by providing the answer right between the bookends of the passage.

"[The grace of God] educates us so that we can live sensible, ethical, and godly lives right now by rejecting ungodly lives and the desires of this world" (Titus 2:12).

With all that we have learned in this study together about ways to await the already, Paul captures it beautifully with three simple words that ought to characterize the life of every follower of Jesus. Our enduring task is to pursue holiness in the present moment, marked by a life that is *sensible, ethical,* and *godly.* Paul chooses those three words carefully, so we should pay close attention to how he uses them and what they mean.

We'll take a closer look at each of those concepts, but first notice that these three words together capture the full range of the spiritual life. To live sensibly (or "with self-control," as it can also mean) is to live in harmony with one's self. To live ethically means to live in harmony with others. And to live in a godly manner means to live in harmony with God. In just three words, Paul reminds us that every relationship we have deserves our fullest commitment to love and reconciliation. You cannot be fully reconciled to others while being in conflict with God or within yourself. You cannot experience inner peace if there is ongoing disharmony with someone else. And you cannot sense the freedom and joy of being in a relationship with God if you fail to love others as yourself.

No wonder Jesus summarized the commandments this way: "You must love the Lord your God with all your heart, with all your being, and with all your mind. This is the first and greatest commandment. And the second is like it: You must love your neighbor as you love yourself (Matthew 22:37-39). All three dimensions to the spiritual life—God, others, and self—are captured right there. And if we ever need a reminder, we just need to recall the prayer that Jesus taught us to pray: "Forgive us our trespasses, as we forgive those who trespass against us." Reconciling ourselves to others and to God is the chief way we can await the already.

So let's take a closer look at what it means to live a sensible, ethical, and godly life.

The Sensible Life

When we think of the word *sensible*, we might automatically call to mind notions of intelligence, wisdom, or at least good common sense. It's sensible to keep your car filled with gas rather than letting it run to empty. It's sensible to put sunscreen on when you're lounging at the beach. It's sensible to keep an eye on the timer when you have a cake in the oven.

To some degree, it works to consider the word *sensible* in this way, since there is an understood notion of having to deal with bad consequences for our bad choices. Live a sensible life and you'll avoid being stranded, getting sunburned, or eating overcooked cake.

But the word has a broader definition than just living wisely and intelligently. The Greek word for sensible can also be translated as "sober" or "self-controlled," and the noun form means something like "temperance." There's an important dimension of discipline and restraint here. To live with sobriety and self-control means to have a life of balance and moderation in all things. This can have some negative connotations in our society, which tends to value excess. We are not so very far removed from Black Friday, a day when few individuals or companies exercise self-control. But in a culture where overeating and binge drinking are serious problems, a life of moderation is something to strive for even if the advertisers don't want us to believe it. Paul is calling his readers to a better way of life than we find in the culture that surrounds us.

Such a sensible life was upheld as an ideal in the Greco-Roman world. Temperance or self-control was one of the four cardinal virtues of Greek philosophy, along with justice, prudence, and courage. By using this word, Paul is telling his readers that we must adopt lives that even outsiders can recognize as virtuous. We should not indulge worldly desires, such as greed or anger, but exercise restraint and keep our minds on higher things. In these instructions, sandwiched between Jesus' prior arrival and his imminent return, Paul calls Christians to live with wisdom, intelligence, and self-control.

The sensible life is one we can achieve because "the grace of God has appeared" (Titus 2:11). That same grace, the gift of salvation in Christ Jesus, "educates us" so that we might live in this way (2:12). The philosophers saw temperance as a virtue to strive for, but Paul here lifts it up as a gift from God. Because "the grace of God has appeared," we have the knowledge and the ability to live virtuously. This way of living is the very means by which we can find inner harmony despite all the internal forces at war within us. Some of our most primal instincts are harmful: hatred of self and others, guilt, shame, low self-esteem, lingering fears of the unknown. And all of these emotions, when unchecked, can cause deep pain to us and to those around us. The sensible life controls these urges, keeping them from running wild in our hearts. It is the mark of a life restored by the grace of God in Jesus Christ.

It is also the first of three key ways that Paul calls us to await the already.

The Ethical Life

It is not enough simply to live in harmony within ourselves; we must also live in the same way with others. To live an *ethical* life means to live with others for the common good, in common regard for one another. It means to live together according to mutually shared values and principles, so that all within a community have common definitions of right and wrong, moral and immoral, just and unjust.

For Paul, there is only one clear basis for the ethics of Christian community, and it is found in the Greek word he uses for ethical. It can also be translated as "upright," "just," or "righteous." For Paul, our ethics are based on the righteousness of God. We are to live according to the commandments of God, and observe the rules Paul lays out in his pastoral letters that constitute Christian community.

In order to live in peace with one another, we must do the right thing, follow God's commandments, and embody the way and example of Jesus himself. It means taking the high road rather than shortcuts, even though it may be costly to do so. It means living according to the eternal standards of love, self-sacrifice, and generosity rather than one's own selfish agendas.

If living *sensibly* means living with a redeemed interior life, living *ethically* means living with redeemed behavior. It means being free to align our actions with the will of God, rather than being encumbered by sin and saturated by the evil around us. The ethical, righteous life is also therefore a gift, as it is only by the grace of God—which has already appeared in Jesus—that we are empowered to live a life in harmony with others.

The word Paul uses here, "ethical" or "righteous," occurs numerous times throughout the New Testament. What's important for our purposes is to note that the Gospel writers even use the word to describe several characters of Advent, with whom by now we are quite familiar.

- In Matthew 1:19, Joseph is called a "righteous" man (same Greek word). He was planning to send Mary away privately when he heard of her pregnancy, because he didn't want to humiliate her. This would have been a justifiable, socially acceptable course of action according to the ethical standards of his culture. But his righteousness was based on a different standard, which was the way of God. And when the angel showed him a different way, Joseph's choice, while difficult, was clear: Observe the commandments of God that had been revealed to him.

- In Luke 1:6, Zechariah and Elizabeth are both called "righteous before God, blameless in their observance of all the Lord's commandments and regulations." And again, they were faced with a choice between cultural expectations and the commandment of God. When their son was born, they were pressured by family and friends to follow the usual custom of naming him after Zechariah. It would have been understandable and acceptable to do so. However, they followed God's will, named him John, and embodied the kind of righteous living Paul calls for in Titus.

- Finally, in Luke 1:17, the work of John the Baptist is characterized as turning "the disobedient to righteous patterns of thinking." His role as a predecessor to Jesus was to prepare the way of upright and just living that would become the standard for all followers of Christ. He would also run counter to the culture at large, not only in the way he dressed and in the foods he ate, but

in his message. By what he preached, he would upset
people in high authority, challenge the priorities of
human relationships ("he will turn the hearts of fathers
back to their children"), and "bring many Israelites back
to the Lord their God" (Luke 1:16-17).

The concept of righteous living is not only central to
Paul's letter to Titus. It is a unifying thread for many of the
characters in the Christmas story, and it serves as a convenient
review for the journey that we have taken this Advent season.
But most importantly, it is a key ingredient for living faithfully
in the present moment, between the Incarnation and the
Second Coming.

The Godly Life

We now turn our attention to the final characteristic of
the faithful life, and in many ways it is the most important.
Paul tells us that we must live *godly* lives. Without a full and
wholehearted devotion to God, one cannot be at peace with
oneself (the *sensible* life) or with others (the *ethical* life).
Godly living is the lynchpin that holds all three together; it
directs our attention and prioritizes all other aspects of our
being to God, recognizing that since God is the giver of life,
God must be the recipient of praise. And if the sensible and
ethical life center on the mind (understanding) and body
(behavior) respectively, then godly living is a matter of the
soul: a soul directed toward the very God whose image and
breath brought it to life.

The word *godly* in Greek is closely related to the word
meaning "to worship." To live a godly life does not simply
mean honoring God because the law requires it, or because

it is customary for Christians to do so, or because we will be punished if we don't. The godly life is one characterized by worship. It is constantly offering good worship, seeking to praise and honor God in every moment of our lives.

Another way to understand the word is *piously*, although that word often conjures up images of cloistered monks huddled in a monastery, or a starched shirt altruist who is completely separated from the realities of real life. It is the same reason we often shun the concept of *saints* and *holiness* when it comes to describing followers of Jesus. We know ourselves all too well, and our imperfections are much too evident even to begin thinking we can live pious, let alone godly, lives.

But the word *godly* does not mean divine, and it does not mean perfect. Instead, it calls us to direct our "good worship" to the One who is. Once we remember that we are not God, we can recalibrate the entirety of our being to the only one who deserves our honor and devotion. The godly life is a life of worship, and in a sense this links back to what we discovered back in Mark about the sacramental life.

While none of the Advent characters are described with this word, it is interesting to see the two people in the Book of Acts who are. The first is Cornelius, and the second is Cornelius' soldier, both in Acts 10 (verses 2 and 7). What is significant about these men is that neither of them were Jews, and Cornelius and his household became the first Gentiles to convert to Christianity (Acts 10:44-48). This story comes right on the heels of the apostle Peter's dramatic vision of the descending sheet, in which he was instructed by God to extend the message of Jesus Christ across cultural and ethnic barriers (Acts 10:9-16).

The godly Cornelius received a vision from God, which turned out to correspond to Peter's own vision in a completely different city. Both visions enlarged and expanded the reach of God's kingdom in the world. They broke through old, preconceived notions about the nature and work of God, as well as divisive barriers that separated people from each other, in order to bring people who had once been separated into God's new covenant together.

Godly living means that you not only offer "good worship" to God as a manner of life, but that you are also open to being used by God to share the message of Christ to those in need. After all, the heart of the Christmas message is that Christ himself, being godly in the purest sense, came into the world to become the very means through which all of us—cast down by sin and separated from God—might be restored to a right relationship with God.

To be a people of Advent means that we share in that same task: to bring people into a transforming experience with God, that they might become godly people themselves.

Our Advent Journey

Our Advent tour through the four Gospels, and this Epistle, has given us a panoramic view of some amazing Christmas vistas. We have witnessed the urgency of John the Baptist's message to prepare ourselves for the coming of Jesus. We have faced the cold, hard reality of Matthew's depiction of life, and emerged more confident because of a God who is here in the midst of it. We have warmed up our vocal chords and sung to the musical score of Luke's Gospel, amazed by the uplifting power of the good news. And in John, we have dared to hold a candle of hope against the darkness of the world.

Four gospels, four perspectives, four portraits of the coming of Christ. And just like waiting for pictures to develop, this Advent season has been filled with expectation, waiting for that moment when we can not just remember, but dynamically relive the arrival of a Christ who is already here.

And how should we await the already?

- By slowing down, turning our lives around, and making a straight path for Jesus to come into our midst.
- By trusting God in the midst of our fears, and learning to experience God's presence in every moment.
- By singing a song of obedience, both to be blessed by God and to be used by God to be a blessing for the world.
- By claiming the light of God, which we may sometimes see most clearly in the midst of our darkness, and reflecting that light for others.
- By living sensible, ethical, and godly lives, wholly devoting ourselves for God's purpose.

Then, slowly and surely, you can watch those pictures develop, right before your eyes. And there you will see Jesus, in the splendor of his majesty and the fullness of his humanity, revealed for you in glorious color.

Reflection Questions:

1. Recall the Christmas letters you have received from family and friends this year. You might even include one that you yourself sent to others. What are the commonalities among the letters? What do they celebrate? What emotions and thoughts to they evoke in you?

2. Why are letters like these so poignant this time of year?

3. Can you identify moments in your past when you experienced that "the grace of God has appeared" in your life? Were those moments in any way turning points in your life? What is helpful about remembering those moments now?

4. In what ways are you awaiting the "blessed hope and the glorious appearance of our great God and Savior Jesus Christ?"

Digging Deeper:

1. Consider the three characteristics of the faithful follower of Jesus: sensible, ethical, and godly. Can you think of anyone you know who embodies one or more of those qualities? Is there anyone who embodies all three?

2. Why is it important to strive for all three of those qualities, rather than simply picking and choosing which of them come most easily for us to fulfill?

Awaiting the Already:

This chapter's investigation into the deeper meanings of *sensible*, *ethical*, and *godly* lend themselves to the personal, practical expression of those characteristics in each of our lives. What can you do differently, starting today, to practice each of these three qualities more in your daily living?

Prayer:

Gracious and eternal God, we thank you for what you have done in the past, and what you will do in the future. As our Advent journey draws to a close, grant us fitness of mind, disciplined behavior, and a passionate spirit to worship you in every present moment. Amen.

CPSIA information can be obtained
at www.ICGtesting.com
Printed in the USA
FSOW02n1352161017
39956FS

9 781501 800894